THIS BOOK BELONGS TO

START DATE

SHE READS TRUTH

## EXECUTIVE

FOUNDER/CHIEF EXECUTIVE OFFICER
Raechel Myers

CO-FOUNDER/CHIEF CONTENT OFFICER
Amanda Bible Williams

CHIEF OPERATING OFFICER
Ryan Myers

EXECUTIVE ASSISTANT
Sarah Andereck

## EDITORIAL

EDITORIAL DIRECTOR
Jessica Lamb

CONTENT EDITOR
Kara Gause

ASSOCIATE EDITORS
Bailey Gillespie
Tameshia Williams

EDITORIAL ASSISTANT
Hannah Little

## CREATIVE

CREATIVE DIRECTOR
Jeremy Mitchell

LEAD DESIGNER
Kelsea Allen

DESIGNERS
Abbey Benson
Davis DeLisi
Annie Glover

## MARKETING

MARKETING DIRECTOR
Krista Juline Williams

MARKETING MANAGER
Katie Matuska Pierce

SOCIAL MEDIA MANAGER
Ansley Rushing

COMMUNITY SUPPORT SPECIALIST
Margot Williams

## SHIPPING & LOGISTICS

LOGISTICS MANAGER
Lauren Gloyne

SHIPPING MANAGER
Sydney Bess

CUSTOMER SUPPORT SPECIALIST
Katy McKnight

FULFILLMENT SPECIALISTS
Abigail Achord
Cait Baggerman

SUBSCRIPTION INQUIRIES
orders@shereadstruth.com

## CONTRIBUTORS

PHOTOGRAPHY
Rachel Dwyer (6, 14, 15, 16, 21, 28, 32, 36, 43, 46, 51, 58, 63, 70, 77, 85, 91, 94, 98, 105, 110)

TEXTILES
Dylan Oglesby

@SHEREADSTRUTH

Download the
She Reads Truth app,
available for iOS
and Android

Subscribe to the
She Reads Truth podcast

SHEREADSTRUTH.COM

---

SHE READS TRUTH™



ISBN 978-1-952670-14-5

1 2 3 4 5 6 7 8 9 10



Verses omitted in the CSB are also omitted in this book.

Research support provided by Logos Bible Software™. Learn more at logos.com.

Though the dates and locations in this book have been carefully researched, scholars disagree on the dating and locations of many biblical events.

This book was printed offset in Nashville, Tennessee, on 70# Lynx Opaque. Cover is 100# Cougar Opaque with a soft touch lamination.

# MARK

REPENT & BELIEVE

SHE READS TRUTH

*The Gospel of Mark is personal,
and it is for every person.*

Raechel Myers
FOUNDER & CHIEF EXECUTIVE OFFICER

In March of 2020, our family decided to read the book of Mark together every morning. In a time when everything about life felt acutely fragile and out of sorts, reading about Jesus became an important daily anchor point for my husband, our two kids, and me.

We started our pandemic days in the living room with a fire (gas log, not real wood, lest you think it was too idyllic) and blankets, our Bibles and journals. Every morning, we took turns reading one chapter out loud. And while my (erroneous) expectation was that my husband and I would be the ones with all of the great insights and observations to offer, I was surprised at what a privilege it was to witness two young hearts and minds experience this Gospel for the first time. They noticed details, asked good questions, and got excited by stories that had become more commonplace to me. It was kind of like taking a friend to a favorite old restaurant and watching them experience the food and flavors for the very first time. But why wouldn't I expect this? That book was written for them, to them, and about the Savior who came to give His life as a ransom for theirs!

The Gospel of Mark is personal, and it is for every person. If you've read it before: good! Read it again. (And again and again and again.) This is your chance to notice new things, draw deeper connections, and be led once more to the cross of Jesus. Or, if this is your first time reading Mark straight through, you are right on time! Don't be afraid to ask questions and dig into the details. And yes, expect the Holy Spirit to carry you to the cross as well—to the feet of your Savior.

As I'm writing this letter, it has been nearly a year since we began that season of reading Mark those mornings in our living room. I read it again this weekend as a refresher, and I am happy (and not at all surprised!) to report that the Word of God in Mark is alive and well one pandemic year later. And, praise the Lord, the Spirit continues to be at work in the heart of this reader.

Friends, our team created this Study Book with an immense amount of care, so that whether Mark is your most beloved book of the Bible or this is your first introduction, this season of reading will be a special one. Every day you'll encounter the Savior who forgives sins, heals bodies, pursues the marginalized, and changes our hearts and our minds. After all, this book was written for *you*, to *you*, and about the Savior who gave His life as a ransom for *yours*.

At She Reads Truth, we believe in pairing the inherently beautiful Word of God with the aesthetic beauty it deserves. Each of our resources is thoughtfully and artfully designed to highlight the beauty, goodness, and truth of Scripture in a way that reflects the themes of each curated reading plan.

For this Study Book, we photographed the process and results of indigo-dyeing fabric as the focal point of our design. When immersed in the indigo dye, fabric is permanently changed. This mirrors both the stories in Mark and our experience today—those who encounter Jesus are forever changed.

*Scan this QR code for a behind-the-scenes video of our Mark photo shoot.*

# INDIGO

## *DYE TUTORIAL*

---

### *SUPPLIES*

Cotton or other non-synthetic fabric
Dye vat
Gloves
150g soda ash
75g sodium hydrosulfite
30g pre-reduced indigo

*No. 1* — *If you want to give your end product a pattern or tie-dye design, use rubber bands, string, or clamps to create the desired effect.*

*No. 2* — *Soak your fabric in water, making sure it is completely wet.*

*No. 3* — *Add soda ash, sodium hydrosulfite, and pre-reduced indigo to the dye vat. The dye will only be effective and active for about thirty minutes, so be prepared to work quickly!*

*No. 4* — *Wearing gloves, dip your fabric in the dye vat. Stir it around to ensure even color saturation, and try to avoid making bubbles.*

*No. 5* — *Pull your fabric out of the dye. If the dye is working, it will appear slightly green. Hang it up and watch as the dye oxidizes and rapidly turns blue. Leave it hanging for a couple of minutes.*

*No. 6* — *Repeat steps 4 and 5 a few more times to achieve a dark indigo blue. The more times you repeat, the darker it will become. (Most denim has been dipped around fifteen times.)*

*No. 7* — *Once you're happy with the color, give your pieces a good rinse in the sink until the water runs mostly clear. Then wash and dry fabric. Be mindful that the color will bleed a bit on a first wash.*

## HOW TO USE THIS BOOK

She Reads Truth is a community of women dedicated to reading the Word of God every day. The Bible is living and active, and we confidently hold it higher than anything we can do or say.

### READ & REFLECT

This **Mark** Study Book focuses primarily on Scripture, with bonus resources to facilitate deeper engagement with God's Word.

SCRIPTURE READING

Designed for a Monday start, this Study Book presents the book of Mark in daily readings, with supplemental passages for additional context.

REFLECTION

Each week ends with space for notes and prompts for reflection.

### COMMUNITY & CONVERSATION

Join women from Manly, IA, to Malaysia as they read with you!

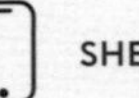

**SHE READS TRUTH APP**

Devotionals corresponding to each daily reading can be found in the **Mark** reading plan on the She Reads Truth app. You can also participate in community discussions, download free lock screens for Weekly Truth memorization, and more.

GRACE DAY

Use Saturdays to catch up on your reading, pray, and rest in the presence of the Lord.

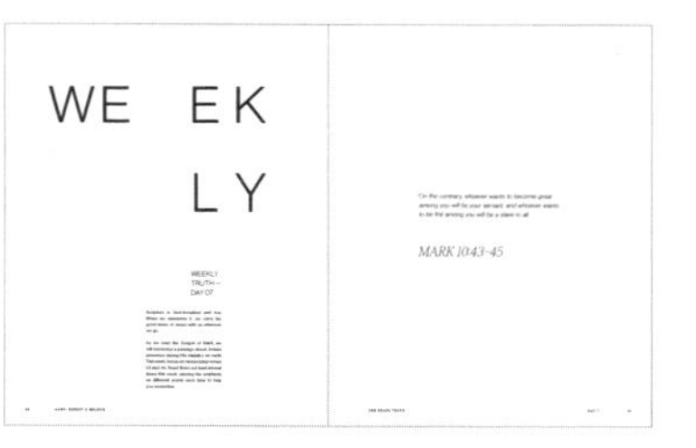


WEEKLY TRUTH

Sundays are set aside for Scripture memorization.

EXTRAS

This book features additional tools to help you gain a deeper understanding of the text.

*See a complete list of extras on page 11.*

**SHEREADSTRUTH.COM**

All of our reading plans and devotionals are also available at SheReadsTruth.com. Invite your family, friends, and neighbors to read along with you!

**SHE READS TRUTH PODCAST**

Join our She Reads Truth founders and their guests each Monday as they open their Bibles and talk about the beauty, goodness, and truth they find there. Subscribe to the podcast so you don't miss conversations about the current community reading plan.

# TABLE *of* CONTENTS

## *WEEK 01*



## *WEEK 02*

# *WEEK 03*



# *EXTRAS*

# KE Y

# VER SE

"FOR EVEN THE SON OF MAN DID NOT COME TO BE SERVED, BUT TO SERVE, AND TO GIVE HIS LIFE AS A RANSOM FOR MANY."

# *She Reads Mark*

## ON THE TIMELINE

Most Bible scholars are convinced Mark was the earliest Gospel written and that it served as one of the sources for the writing of Matthew and Luke. It is believed Mark wrote his Gospel between AD 64–68. The events in the Gospel of Mark take place during Jesus's ministry (around AD 30 to 33).

## A LITTLE BACKGROUND

The Gospel of Mark is anonymous, though the author is believed to be John Mark. He was the son of a widow named Mary, in whose house the church in Jerusalem sometimes gathered (Ac 12:12–17) and where Jesus possibly ate the Last Supper with His disciples.

According to the early Church fathers, Mark wrote his Gospel in Rome either just before or soon after Peter's martyrdom. Because Mark wrote primarily for Roman Gentiles, he explained Jewish customs, translated Aramaic words and phrases into Greek, used Latin terms rather than their Greek equivalents, and rarely quoted from the Old Testament.

## MESSAGE AND PURPOSE

Mark's Gospel is a narrative about Jesus, and Mark identified this theme in the first verse of the book: "the gospel of Jesus Christ, the Son of God." The major emphasis of Mark's Gospel is that Jesus is the divine Son of God, as announced by God at Jesus's baptism (Mk 1:9–11). Demons and unclean spirits recognized and acknowledged Jesus's divinity in Mark 3:11 and 5:7, and God reaffirmed it at the transfiguration in Mark 9:7. Jesus taught it parabolically in Mark 12:1–12, hinted at it in 13:32, and confessed it directly in 14:61–62. Finally, a Roman centurion confessed it openly and without qualification in Mark 15:39. Mark's purpose was to summon people to repent and believe the good news of Jesus Christ, the Messiah, the Son of God (Mk 1:1, 15).

## GIVE THANKS FOR THE GOSPEL OF MARK

Many individuals in Jesus's day laid claim to the title of Messiah. The Gospel of Mark clarifies the nature of the true Messiah and redefines the title in light of Jesus's life, death, and resurrection. Mark also gives us a strong picture of how Jesus is both human and divine, with special emphasis on His humanity and emotions.

# NARRATIVE INTERRUPTIONS *in* MARK

This symbol will denote each Markan sandwich in the margins of your daily reading.

One of the distinctive literary features of Mark's Gospel is his frequent interrupting of one story to insert a second story in the middle. These "Markan sandwiches" have a purpose: to help us understand one story by connecting it to another. Each instance is marked in the margins of your daily reading. As you read, notice how one story illustrates or clarifies the other.

| | |
|---|---|
| MARK 3:20–35 | MARK 4:1–20 |
| MARK 5:21–43 | MARK 11:12–25 |
| MARK 14:1–11 | MARK 14:17–31 |

"THE KINGDOM OF GOD HAS COME NEAR."

# THE KINGDOM OF GOD COMES NEAR

## *DAY 01*

*As you read Mark 1–6, you'll see many different people and groups encountering Jesus. Use the space provided on page 40 to make notes on how each group or person responded to Him.*

### MARK 1

#### THE MESSIAH'S HERALD

[1] The beginning of the gospel of Jesus Christ, the Son of God. [2] As it is written in Isaiah the prophet:

See, I am sending my messenger ahead of you;
he will prepare your way.
[3] A voice of one crying out in the wilderness:
Prepare the way for the Lord;
make his paths straight!

[4] John came baptizing in the wilderness and proclaiming a baptism of repentance for the forgiveness of sins. [5] The whole Judean countryside and all the people of Jerusalem were going out to him, and they were baptized by him in the Jordan River, confessing their sins. [6] John wore a camel-hair garment with a leather belt around his waist and ate locusts and wild honey.

[7] He proclaimed, "One who is more powerful than I am is coming after me. I am not worthy to stoop down and untie the strap of his sandals. [8] I baptize you with water, but he will baptize you with the Holy Spirit."

#### THE BAPTISM OF JESUS

[9] In those days Jesus came from Nazareth in Galilee and was baptized in the Jordan by John. [10] As soon as he came up out of the water, he saw the heavens being torn open and the Spirit descending on him like a dove. [11] And a voice came from heaven: "You are my beloved Son; with you I am well-pleased."

### THE TEMPTATION OF JESUS

[12] Immediately the Spirit drove him into the wilderness. [13] He was in the wilderness forty days, being tempted by Satan. He was with the wild animals, and the angels were serving him.

### MINISTRY IN GALILEE

[14] After John was arrested, Jesus went to Galilee, proclaiming the good news of God: [15] "The time is fulfilled, and the kingdom of God has come near. Repent and believe the good news!"

### THE FIRST DISCIPLES

[16] As he passed alongside the Sea of Galilee, he saw Simon and Andrew, Simon's brother, casting a net into the sea—for they were fishermen. [17] "Follow me," Jesus told them, "and I will make you fish for people." [18] Immediately they left their nets and followed him. [19] Going on a little farther, he saw James the son of Zebedee and his brother John in a boat putting their nets in order. [20] Immediately he called them, and they left their father Zebedee in the boat with the hired men and followed him.

### DRIVING OUT AN UNCLEAN SPIRIT

[21] They went into Capernaum, and right away he entered the synagogue on the Sabbath and began to teach. [22] They were astonished at his teaching because he was teaching them as one who had authority, and not like the scribes.

[23] Just then a man with an unclean spirit was in their synagogue. He cried out, [24] "What do you have to do with us, Jesus of Nazareth? Have you come to destroy us? I know who you are—the Holy One of God!"

[25] Jesus rebuked him saying, "Be silent, and come out of him!" [26] And the unclean spirit threw him into convulsions, shouted with a loud voice, and came out of him.

[27] They were all amazed, and so they began to ask each other, "What is this? A new teaching with authority! He commands even the unclean spirits, and they obey him." [28] At once the news about him spread throughout the entire vicinity of Galilee.

### HEALINGS AT CAPERNAUM

[29] As soon as they left the synagogue, they went into Simon and Andrew's house with James and John. [30] Simon's mother-in-law was lying in bed with a fever, and they told him about her at once. [31] So he went to her, took her by the hand, and raised her up. The fever left her, and she began to serve them.

[32] When evening came, after the sun had set, they brought to him all those who were sick and demon-possessed. [33] The whole town was assembled at the door, [34] and he healed many who were sick with various diseases and drove out many demons. And he would not permit the demons to speak, because they knew him.

### PREACHING IN GALILEE

[35] Very early in the morning, while it was still dark, he got up, went out, and made his way to a deserted place; and there he was praying. [36] Simon and his companions searched for him, [37] and when they found him they said, "Everyone is looking for you."

[38] And he said to them, "Let's go on to the neighboring villages so that I may preach there too. This is why I have come."

### A MAN CLEANSED

[39] He went into all of Galilee, preaching in their synagogues and driving out demons. [40] Then a man with leprosy came to him and, on his knees, begged him, "If you are willing, you can make me clean." [41] Moved with compassion, Jesus reached out his hand and touched him. "I am willing," he told him. "Be made clean." [42] Immediately the leprosy left him, and he was made clean. [43] Then he sternly warned him and sent him away at once, [44] telling him, "See that you say nothing to anyone; but go and show yourself to the priest, and offer what Moses commanded for your cleansing, as a testimony to them." [45] Yet he went out and began to proclaim it widely and to spread the news, with the result that Jesus could no longer enter a town openly. But he was out in deserted places, and they came to him from everywhere.

## NAHUM 1:15

Look to the mountains—
the feet of the herald,
who proclaims peace.
Celebrate your festivals, Judah;
fulfill your vows.
For the wicked one will never again
march through you;
he will be entirely wiped out.

## MALACHI 3:1

"See, I am going to send my messenger, and he will clear the way before me. Then the Lord you seek will suddenly come to his temple, the Messenger of the covenant you delight in—see, he is coming," says the LORD of Armies.

DAY 02

# JESUS FORGIVES AND HEALS

## MARK 2

### THE SON OF MAN FORGIVES AND HEALS

[1] When he entered Capernaum again after some days, it was reported that he was at home. [2] So many people gathered together that there was no more room, not even in the doorway, and he was speaking the word to them. [3] They came to him bringing a paralytic, carried by four of them. [4] Since they were not able to bring him to Jesus because of the crowd, they removed the roof above him, and after digging through it, they lowered the mat on which the paralytic was lying.

*[5] Seeing their faith, Jesus told the paralytic, "Son, your sins are forgiven."*

[6] But some of the scribes were sitting there, questioning in their hearts: [7] "Why does he speak like this? He's blaspheming! Who can forgive sins but God alone?"

[8] Right away Jesus perceived in his spirit that they were thinking like this within themselves and said to them, "Why are you thinking these things in your hearts? [9] Which is easier: to say to the paralytic, 'Your sins are forgiven,' or to say, 'Get up, take your mat, and walk'? [10] But so that you may know that the Son of Man has authority on earth to forgive sins"—he told the paralytic— [11] "I tell you: get up, take your mat, and go home."

[12] Immediately he got up, took the mat, and went out in front of everyone. As a result, they were all astounded and gave glory to God, saying, "We have never seen anything like this!"

### THE CALL OF LEVI

[13] Jesus went out again beside the sea. The whole crowd was coming to him, and he was teaching them. [14] Then, passing by, he saw Levi the son of Alphaeus sitting at the tax office, and he said to him, "Follow me," and he got up and followed him.

[15] While he was reclining at the table in Levi's house, many tax collectors and sinners were eating with Jesus and his disciples, for there were many who were following him. [16] When the scribes who were Pharisees saw that he was eating with sinners and tax collectors, they asked his disciples, "Why does he eat with tax collectors and sinners?"

[17] When Jesus heard this, he told them, "It is not those who are well who need a doctor, but those who are sick.

*I didn't come to call the righteous, but sinners."*

A QUESTION ABOUT FASTING

[18] Now John's disciples and the Pharisee were fasting. People came and asked him, "Why do John's disciples and the Pharisees' disciples fast, but your disciples do not fast?"

[19] Jesus said to them, "The wedding guests cannot fast while the groom is with them, can they? As long as they have the groom with them, they cannot fast. [20] But the time will come when the groom will be taken away from them, and then they will fast on that day. [21] No one sews a patch of unshrunk cloth on an old garment. Otherwise, the new patch pulls away from the old cloth, and a worse tear is made. [22] And no one puts new wine into old wineskins. Otherwise, the wine will burst the skins, and the wine is lost as well as the skins. No, new wine is put into fresh wineskins."

LORD OF THE SABBATH

[23] On the Sabbath he was going through the grainfields, and his disciples began to make their way, picking some heads of grain. [24] The Pharisees said to him, "Look, why are they doing what is not lawful on the Sabbath?"

[25] He said to them, "Have you never read what David and those who were with him did when he was in need and hungry — [26] how he entered the house of God in the time of Abiathar the high priest and ate the bread of the Presence —which is not lawful for anyone to eat except the priests —and also gave some to his companions?" [27] Then he told them, "The Sabbath was made for man and not man for the Sabbath. [28] So then, the Son of Man is Lord even of the Sabbath."

## MARK 3

[1] Jesus entered the synagogue again, and a man was there who had a shriveled hand. [2] In order to accuse him, they were watching him closely to see whether he would heal him on the Sabbath. [3] He told the man with the shriveled hand, "Stand before us." [4] Then he said to them, "Is it lawful to do good on the Sabbath or to do evil, to save life or to kill?" But they were silent. [5] After looking around at them with anger, he was grieved at the hardness of their hearts and told the man, "Stretch out your hand." So he stretched it out, and his hand was restored. [6] Immediately the Pharisees went out and started plotting with the Herodians against him, how they might kill him.

MINISTERING TO THE MULTITUDE

[7] Jesus departed with his disciples to the sea, and a large crowd followed from Galilee, and a large crowd followed from Judea, [8] Jerusalem, Idumea, beyond the Jordan, and around Tyre and Sidon.

*The large crowd came to him because they heard about everything he was doing.*

[9] Then he told his disciples to have a small boat ready for him, so that the crowd wouldn't crush him. [10] Since he had healed many, all who had diseases were pressing toward him to touch him. [11] Whenever the unclean spirits saw him, they fell down before him and cried out, "You are the Son of God!" [12] And he would strongly warn them not to make him known.

THE TWELVE APOSTLES

[13] Jesus went up the mountain and summoned those he wanted, and they came to him. [14] He appointed twelve, whom he also named apostles, to be with him, to send them out to preach, [15] and to have authority to drive out demons. [16] He appointed the Twelve: To Simon, he gave the name Peter; [17] and to James the son of Zebedee, and to his brother John, he gave the name "Boanerges" (that is, "Sons of Thunder"); [18] Andrew; Philip and Bartholomew; Matthew and Thomas; James the son of Alphaeus, and Thaddaeus; Simon the Zealot, [19] and Judas Iscariot, who also betrayed him.

A HOUSE DIVIDED

[20] Jesus entered a house, and the crowd gathered again so that they were not even able to eat. [21] When his family heard this, they set out to restrain him, because they said, "He's out of his mind."

[22] The scribes who had come down from Jerusalem said, "He is possessed by Beelzebul," and, "He drives out demons by the ruler of the demons."

[23] So he summoned them and spoke to them in parables: "How can Satan drive out Satan? [24] If a kingdom is divided against itself, that kingdom cannot stand. [25] If a house is divided against itself, that house cannot stand. [26] And if Satan opposes himself and is divided, he cannot stand but is finished. [27] But no one can enter a strong man's house and plunder his possessions unless he first ties up the strong man. Then he can plunder his house.

[28] "Truly I tell you, people will be forgiven for all sins and whatever blasphemies they utter. [29] But whoever blasphemes against the Holy Spirit never has forgiveness, but is guilty of an eternal sin"— [30] because they were saying, "He has an unclean spirit."

## MARKAN SANDWICH

*MARK 3:20–35*

**Opens with**

Jesus gathering a crowd at a house, and His family accusing Him of being out of His mind.

**Shifts to**

Jesus sharing a parable of how a house divided against itself cannot stand.

**Returns to**

Jesus's mother and brothers arriving, and Jesus referring to the crowd as His family.

TRUE RELATIONSHIPS

[31] His mother and his brothers came, and standing outside, they sent word to him and called him. [32] A crowd was sitting around him and told him, "Look, your mother, your brothers, and your sisters are outside asking for you."

[33] He replied to them, "Who are my mother and my brothers?" [34] Looking at those sitting in a circle around him, he said, "Here are my mother and my brothers! [35] Whoever does the will of God is my brother and sister and mother."

## 1 SAMUEL 21:1–6

DAVID FLEES TO NOB

[1] David went to the priest Ahimelech at Nob. Ahimelech was afraid to meet David, so he said to him, "Why are you alone and no one is with you?"

[2] David answered the priest Ahimelech, "The king gave me a mission, but he told me, 'Don't let anyone know anything about the mission I'm sending you on or what I have ordered you to do.' I have stationed my young men at a certain place. [3] Now what do you have on hand? Give me five loaves of bread or whatever can be found."

[4] The priest told him, "There is no ordinary bread on hand. However, there is consecrated bread, but the young men may eat it only if they have kept themselves from women."

[5] David answered him, "I swear that women are being kept from us, as always when I go out to battle. The young men's bodies are consecrated even on an ordinary mission, so of course their bodies are consecrated today." [6] So the priest gave him the consecrated bread, for there was no bread there except the Bread of the Presence that had been removed from the presence of the LORD. When the bread was removed, it had been replaced with warm bread.

## HEBREWS 2:11–12

[11] For the one who sanctifies and those who are sanctified all have one Father. That is why Jesus is not ashamed to call them brothers and sisters, [12] saying:

> I will proclaim your name to my brothers and sisters;
> I will sing hymns to you in the congregation.

# JESUS'S MINISTRY AROUND *the* SEA *of* GALILEE

Jesus walked, talked, and interacted with the people around Him. This map provides an up-close look at the region around the Sea of Galilee where several moments of Jesus's ministry occurred.

1. Jesus calls Simon and Andrew, John and James, and Levi.
   *Mk 1:16–20; 2:13–14*
2. Jesus teaches and heals.
   *Mk 1:21–34; 2:1–5; 9:33–37*
3. Jesus calms the storm.
   *Mk 4:35–41*
4. Jesus feeds the multitudes.
   *Mk 6:30–44*
5. Jesus appears to His disciples on the sea.
   *Mk 6:45–52*
6. Jesus is recognized by crowds who seek and receive healing.
   *Mk 6:53–56*
7. Jesus heals a blind man.
   *Mk 8:22–26*
8. Jesus is transfigured.
   *Mk 9:2–8*

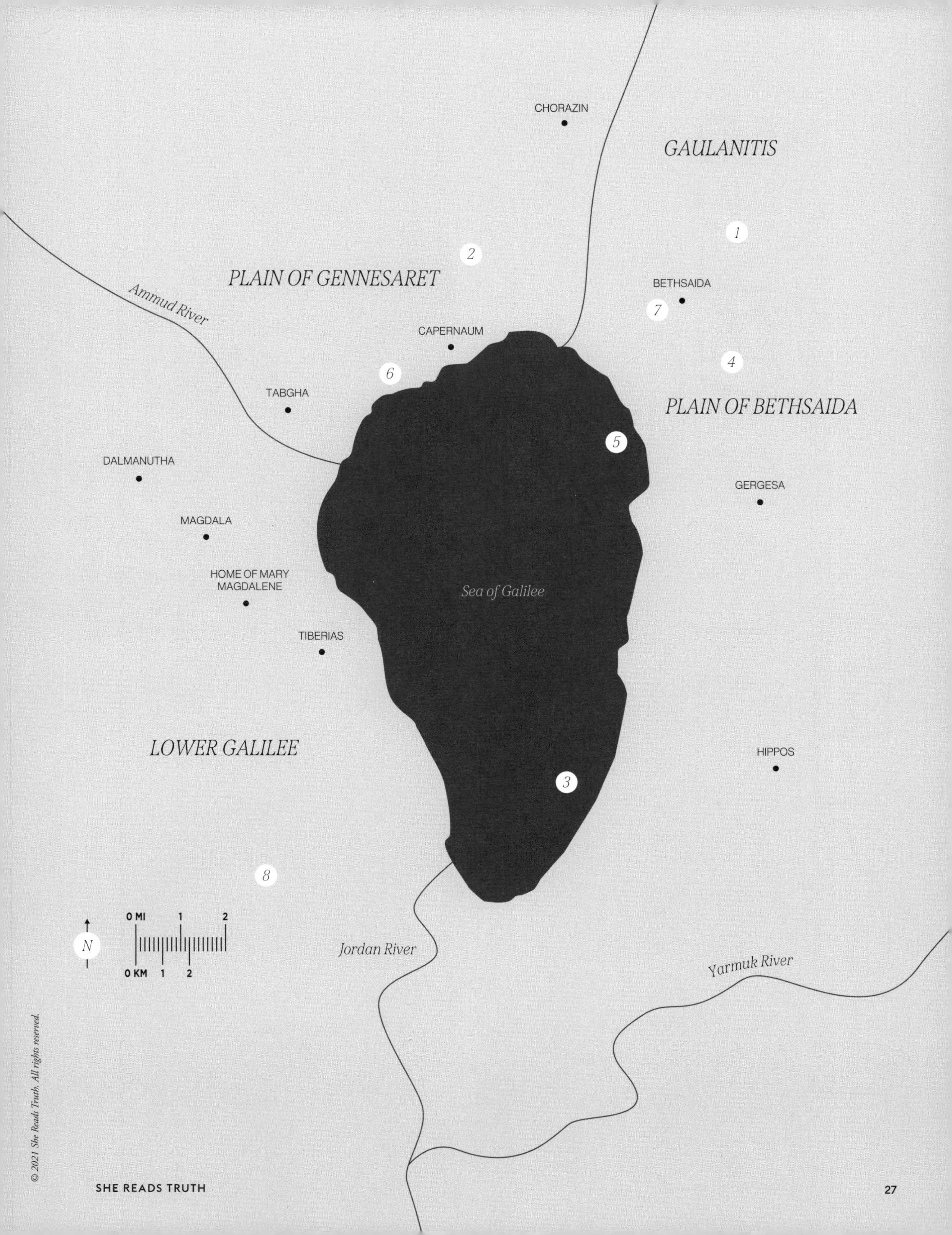
CHORAZIN
GAULANITIS
1
2
PLAIN OF GENNESARET
BETHSAIDA
7
Ammud River
CAPERNAUM
4
6
TABGHA
PLAIN OF BETHSAIDA
5
DALMANUTHA
GERGESA
MAGDALA
HOME OF MARY MAGDALENE
Sea of Galilee
TIBERIAS
LOWER GALILEE
HIPPOS
3
8
N
0 MI
1
2
0 KM
1
2
Jordan River
Yarmuk River

# THE SEED PARABLES

DAY 03

## MARK 4

### THE PARABLE OF THE SOWER

[1] Again he began to teach by the sea, and a very large crowd gathered around him. So he got into a boat on the sea and sat down, while the whole crowd was by the sea on the shore. [2] He taught them many things in parables, and in his teaching he said to them, [3] "Listen! Consider the sower who went out to sow. [4] As he sowed, some seed fell along the path, and the birds came and devoured it. [5] Other seed fell on rocky ground where it didn't have much soil, and it grew up quickly, since the soil wasn't deep. [6] When the sun came up, it was scorched, and since it had no root, it withered away. [7] Other seed fell among thorns, and the thorns came up and choked it, and it didn't produce fruit. [8] Still other seed fell on good ground and it grew up, producing fruit that increased thirty, sixty, and a hundred times." [9] Then he said, "Let anyone who has ears to hear listen."

### WHY JESUS USED PARABLES

[10] When he was alone, those around him with the Twelve asked him about the parables. [11] He answered them,

*"The secret of the kingdom of God has been given to you,*

but to those outside, everything comes in parables [12] so that

they may indeed look,
and yet not perceive;
they may indeed listen,
and yet not understand;
otherwise, they might turn back
and be forgiven."

### THE PARABLE OF THE SOWER EXPLAINED

[13] Then he said to them, "Don't you understand this parable? How then will you understand all of the parables? [14] The sower sows the word. [15] Some are like the word sown on the path. When they hear, immediately Satan comes and takes away the word sown in them. [16] And others are like seed sown on rocky ground. When they hear the word, immediately they receive it with joy. [17] But they have no root; they are short-lived. When distress or persecution comes because of the word, they immediately fall away. [18] Others are like seed sown among thorns; these are the ones who hear the word, [19] but the worries of this age, the deceitfulness of wealth, and the desires for other things enter in and choke the word, and it becomes unfruitful. [20] And those like seed sown on good ground hear the word, welcome it, and produce fruit thirty, sixty, and a hundred times what was sown."

## MARKAN SANDWICH

*MARK 4:1–20*

**Opens with**

Jesus sharing a parable about a sower.

**Shifts to**

Jesus explaining why He teaches in parables.

**Returns to**

Jesus explaining the meaning of the parable of the sower.

USING YOUR LIGHT

[21] He also said to them, "Is a lamp brought in to be put under a basket or under a bed? Isn't it to be put on a lampstand? [22] For there is nothing hidden that will not be revealed, and nothing concealed that will not be brought to light. [23] If anyone has ears to hear, let him listen."

## *[24] And he said to them, "Pay attention to what you hear.*

By the measure you use, it will be measured to you—and more will be added to you. [25] For whoever has, more will be given to him, and whoever does not have, even what he has will be taken away from him."

THE PARABLE OF THE GROWING SEED

[26] "The kingdom of God is like this," he said. "A man scatters seed on the ground. [27] He sleeps and rises night and day; the seed sprouts and grows, although he doesn't know how. [28] The soil produces a crop by itself—first the blade, then the head, and then the full grain on the head. [29] As soon as the crop is ready, he sends for the sickle, because the harvest has come."

THE PARABLE OF THE MUSTARD SEED

[30] And he said, "With what can we compare the kingdom of God, or what parable can we use to describe it? [31] It's like a mustard seed that, when sown upon the soil, is the smallest of all the seeds on the ground. [32] And when sown, it comes up and grows taller than all the garden plants, and produces large branches, so that the birds of the sky can nest in its shade."

USING PARABLES

[33] He was speaking the word to them with many parables like these, as they were able to understand. [34] He did not speak to them without a parable. Privately, however, he explained everything to his own disciples.

WIND AND WAVES OBEY JESUS

[35] On that day, when evening had come, he told them, "Let's cross over to the other side of the sea." [36] So they left the crowd and took him along since he was in the boat. And other boats were with him. [37] A great windstorm arose, and the waves were breaking over the boat, so that the boat was already being swamped. [38] He was in the stern, sleeping on the cushion. So they woke him up and said to him, "Teacher! Don't you care that we're going to die?"

[39] He got up, rebuked the wind, and said to the sea, "Silence! Be still!" The wind ceased, and there was a great calm. [40] Then he said to them, "Why are you afraid? Do you still have no faith?"

[41] And they were terrified and asked one another,

*"Who then is this? Even the wind and the sea obey him!"*

## PROVERBS 2:1–6

### WISDOM'S WORTH

[1] My son, if you accept my words
and store up my commands within you,
[2] listening closely to wisdom
and directing your heart to understanding;
[3] furthermore, if you call out to insight
and lift your voice to understanding,
[4] if you seek it like silver
and search for it like hidden treasure,
[5] then you will understand the fear of the LORD
and discover the knowledge of God.
[6] For the LORD gives wisdom;
from his mouth come knowledge and understanding.

## AMOS 4:13

He is here:
the one who forms the mountains,
creates the wind,
and reveals his thoughts to man,
the one who makes the dawn out of darkness
and strides on the heights of the earth.
The LORD, the God of Armies, is his name.

# JESUS RESCUES, RESTORES, AND HEALS

DAY 04

## MARK 5

### DEMONS DRIVEN OUT BY JESUS

[1] They came to the other side of the sea, to the region of the Gerasenes. [2] As soon as he got out of the boat, a man with an unclean spirit came out of the tombs and met him. [3] He lived in the tombs, and no one was able to restrain him anymore—not even with a chain— [4] because he often had been bound with shackles and chains, but had torn the chains apart and smashed the shackles. No one was strong enough to subdue him. [5] Night and day among the tombs and on the mountains, he was always crying out and cutting himself with stones.

[6] When he saw Jesus from a distance, he ran and knelt down before him. [7] And he cried out with a loud voice, "What do you have to do with me, Jesus, Son of the Most High God? I beg you before God, don't torment me!" [8] For he had told him, "Come out of the man, you unclean spirit!"

[9] "What is your name?" he asked him.

"My name is Legion," he answered him, "because we are many." [10] And he begged him earnestly not to send them out of the region.

[11] A large herd of pigs was there, feeding on the hillside. [12] The demons begged him, "Send us to the pigs, so that we may enter them." [13] So he gave them permission, and the unclean spirits came out and entered the pigs. The herd of about two thousand rushed down the steep bank into the sea and drowned there.

[14] The men who tended them ran off and reported it in the town and the countryside, and people went to see what had happened. [15] They came to Jesus and saw the man who had been demon-possessed, sitting there, dressed and in his right mind; and they were afraid. [16] Those who had seen it described to them what had happened to the demon-possessed man and told about the pigs. [17] Then they began to beg him to leave their region.

[18] As he was getting into the boat, the man who had been demon-possessed begged him earnestly that he might remain with him. [19] Jesus did not let him but told him,

*"Go home to your own people, and report to them how much the Lord has done for you and how he has had mercy on you."*

[20] So he went out and began to proclaim in the Decapolis how much Jesus had done for him, and they were all amazed.

## MARKAN SANDWICH

*MARK 5:21–43*

**Opens with**

Jairus seeking Jesus's help for his dying daughter.

**Shifts to**

a bleeding woman touching Jesus's robe and being healed.

**Returns to**

Jesus healing Jairus's daughter.

A GIRL RESTORED AND A WOMAN HEALED

[21] When Jesus had crossed over again by boat to the other side, a large crowd gathered around him while he was by the sea. [22] One of the synagogue leaders, named Jairus, came, and when he saw Jesus, he fell at his feet [23] and begged him earnestly, "My little daughter is dying.

*Come and lay your hands on her so that she can get well and live."*

[24] So Jesus went with him, and a large crowd was following and pressing against him.

[25] Now a woman suffering from bleeding for twelve years [26] had endured much under many doctors. She had spent everything she had and was not helped at all. On the contrary, she became worse. [27] Having heard about Jesus, she came up behind him in the crowd and touched his clothing. [28] For she said, "If I just touch his clothes, I'll be made well." [29] Instantly her flow of blood ceased, and she sensed in her body that she was healed of her affliction.

[30] Immediately Jesus realized that power had gone out from him. He turned around in the crowd and said, "Who touched my clothes?"

[31] His disciples said to him, "You see the crowd pressing against you, and yet you say, 'Who touched me?'"

[32] But he was looking around to see who had done this. [33] The woman, with fear and trembling, knowing what had happened to her, came and fell down before him, and told him the whole truth. [34] "Daughter," he said to her, "your faith has saved you. Go in peace and be healed from your affliction."

[35] While he was still speaking, people came from the synagogue leader's house and said, "Your daughter is dead. Why bother the teacher anymore?"

[36] When Jesus overheard what was said, he told the synagogue leader, "Don't be afraid. Only believe." [37] He did not let anyone accompany him except Peter, James, and John, James's brother. [38] They came to the leader's house, and he saw a commotion—people weeping and wailing loudly. [39] He went in and said to them, "Why are you making a commotion and weeping? The child is not dead but asleep." [40] They laughed at him, but he put them all outside. He took the child's father, mother, and those who were with him, and entered the place where the child was. [41] Then he took the child by the hand and said to her, "Talitha koum" (which is translated, "Little girl, I say to you, get up"). [42] Immediately the girl

got up and began to walk. (She was twelve years old.) At this they were utterly astounded. [43] Then he gave them strict orders that no one should know about this and told them to give her something to eat.

## ACTS 9:39–41

[39] Peter got up and went with them. When he arrived, they led him to the room upstairs. And all the widows approached him, weeping and showing him the robes and clothes that Dorcas had made while she was with them. [40] Peter sent them all out of the room. He knelt down, prayed, and turning toward the body said, "Tabitha, get up." She opened her eyes, saw Peter, and sat up. [41] He gave her his hand and helped her stand up. He called the saints and widows and presented her alive.

## JAMES 2:19

You believe that God is one. Good! Even the demons believe—and they shudder.

"HAVE COURAGE! IT IS I. DON'T BE AFRAID."

# JESUS WALKS ON WATER

*DAY 05*

MARK 6

REJECTION AT NAZARETH

[1] He left there and came to his hometown, and his disciples followed him. [2] When the Sabbath came, he began to teach in the synagogue, and many who heard him were astonished. "Where did this man get these things?" they said. "What is this wisdom that has been given to him, and how are these miracles performed by his hands? [3] Isn't this the carpenter, the son of Mary, and the brother of James, Joses, Judas, and Simon? And aren't his sisters here with us?" So they were offended by him.

[4] Jesus said to them, "A prophet is not without honor except in his hometown, among his relatives, and in his household." [5] He was not able to do a miracle there, except that he laid his hands on a few sick people and healed them. [6] And he was amazed at their unbelief. He was going around the villages teaching.

COMMISSIONING THE TWELVE

[7] He summoned the Twelve and began to send them out in pairs and gave them authority over unclean spirits. [8] He instructed them to take nothing for the road except a staff—no bread, no traveling bag, no money in their belts, [9] but to wear sandals and not put on an extra shirt. [10] He said to them, "Whenever you enter a house, stay there until you leave that place. [11] If any place does not welcome you or listen to you, when you leave there, shake the dust off your feet as a testimony against them." [12] So they went out and preached that people should repent. [13] They drove out many demons, anointed many sick people with oil and healed them.

### JOHN THE BAPTIST BEHEADED

[14] King Herod heard about it, because Jesus's name had become well known. Some said, "John the Baptist has been raised from the dead, and that's why miraculous powers are at work in him." [15] But others said, "He's Elijah." Still others said, "He's a prophet, like one of the prophets from long ago."

[16] When Herod heard of it, he said, "John, the one I beheaded, has been raised!"

[17] For Herod himself had given orders to arrest John and to chain him in prison on account of Herodias, his brother Philip's wife, because he had married her. [18] John had been telling Herod, "It is not lawful for you to have your brother's wife." [19] So Herodias held a grudge against him and wanted to kill him. But she could not, [20] because Herod feared John and protected him, knowing he was a righteous and holy man. When Herod heard him he would be very perplexed, and yet he liked to listen to him.

[21] An opportune time came on his birthday, when Herod gave a banquet for his nobles, military commanders, and the leading men of Galilee. [22] When Herodias's own daughter came in and danced, she pleased Herod and his guests. The king said to the girl, "Ask me whatever you want, and I'll give it to you." [23] He promised her with an oath: "Whatever you ask me I will give you, up to half my kingdom."

[24] She went out and said to her mother, "What should I ask for?"

"John the Baptist's head," she said.

[25] At once she hurried to the king and said, "I want you to give me John the Baptist's head on a platter immediately." [26] Although the king was deeply distressed, because of his oaths and the guests he did not want to refuse her. [27] The king immediately sent for an executioner and commanded him to bring John's head. So he went and beheaded him in prison, [28] brought his head on a platter, and gave it to the girl. Then the girl gave it to her mother. [29] When John's disciples heard about it, they came and removed his corpse and placed it in a tomb.

### FEEDING OF THE FIVE THOUSAND

[30] The apostles gathered around Jesus and reported to him all that they had done and taught. [31] He said to them, "Come away by yourselves to a remote place and rest for a while." For many people were coming and going, and they did not even have time to eat.

[32] So they went away in the boat by themselves to a remote place, [33] but many saw them leaving and recognized them, and they ran on foot from all the towns and arrived ahead of them.

[34] When he went ashore, he saw a large crowd and had compassion on them, because they were like sheep without a shepherd. Then he began to teach them many things.

[35] When it grew late, his disciples approached him and said, "This place is deserted, and it is already late. [36] Send them away so that they can go into the surrounding countryside and villages to buy themselves something to eat."

[37] "You give them something to eat," he responded.

They said to him, "Should we go and buy two hundred denarii worth of bread and give them something to eat?"

[38] He asked them, "How many loaves do you have? Go and see."

When they found out they said, "Five, and two fish." [39] Then he instructed them to have all the people sit down in groups on the green grass. [40] So they sat down in groups of hundreds and fifties. [41] He took the five loaves and the two fish, and looking up to heaven, he blessed and broke the loaves. He kept giving them to his disciples to set before the people. He also divided the two fish among them all. [42] Everyone ate and was satisfied. [43] They picked up twelve baskets full of pieces of bread and fish. [44] Now those who had eaten the loaves were five thousand men.

#### WALKING ON THE WATER

[45] Immediately he made his disciples get into the boat and go ahead of him to the other side, to Bethsaida, while he dismissed the crowd. [46] After he said good-bye to them, he went away to the mountain to pray. [47] Well into the night, the boat was in the middle of the sea, and he was alone on the land. [48] He saw them straining at the oars, because the wind was against them. Very early in the morning he came toward them walking on the sea and wanted to pass by them. [49] When they saw him walking on the sea, they thought it was a ghost and cried out, [50] because they all saw him and were terrified. Immediately he spoke with them and said, "Have courage! It is I. Don't be afraid." [51] Then he got into the boat with them, and the wind ceased. They were completely astounded, [52] because they had not understood about the loaves. Instead, their hearts were hardened.

#### MIRACULOUS HEALINGS

[53] When they had crossed over, they came to shore at Gennesaret and anchored there.

[54] As they got out of the boat, people immediately recognized him. [55] They hurried throughout that region and began to carry the sick on mats to wherever they heard he was. [56] Wherever he went, into villages, towns, or the country, they laid the sick in the marketplaces and begged him that they might touch just the end of his robe. And everyone who touched it was healed.

### 2 KINGS 2:11

As they continued walking and talking, a chariot of fire with horses of fire suddenly appeared and separated the two of them. Then Elijah went up into heaven in the whirlwind.

### EZEKIEL 34:4–5

[4] "You have not strengthened the weak, healed the sick, bandaged the injured, brought back the strays, or sought the lost. Instead, you have ruled them with violence and cruelty. [5] They were scattered for lack of a shepherd; they became food for all the wild animals when they were scattered."

# WEEK *1*
## *Reflection*

The Gospel of Mark repeatedly illustrates how an encounter with Jesus demands a response. Look back over this week's reading to make notes on how each of the people or groups of people listed below responded to Jesus.

| | |
|---|---|
| JOHN *the* BAPTIST | *DAY 1* |
| JAMES *and* JOHN | *DAY 1* |
| SIMON'S MOTHER-*in*-LAW | *DAY 1* |
| MAN *with* LEPROSY | *DAY 1* |
| FRIENDS *of the* PARALYTIC MAN | *DAY 1* |
| SCRIBES | *DAY 2* |
| PEOPLE *in* CAPERNAUM | *DAY 2* |
| LEVI | *DAY 2* |
| JESUS'S FAMILY | *DAY 2* |
| DEMON-POSSESSED MAN | *DAY 4* |
| JAIRUS | *DAY 4* |
| WOMAN *with a* BLEEDING CONDITION | *DAY 4* |
| PEOPLE *in* NAZARETH | *DAY 5* |
| PEOPLE *in* GENNESARET | *DAY 5* |

MARK 2:17

WHEN JESUS HEARD THIS, HE TOLD THEM, "IT IS NOT THOSE WHO ARE WELL WHO NEED A DOCTOR, BUT THOSE WHO ARE SICK. I DIDN'T COME TO CALL THE RIGHTEOUS, BUT SINNERS."

Reflect on your first encounter with Jesus. In the journaling space below, write about this experience. How did you respond to Him?

GR

Take this day to catch up on your reading, pray, and rest in the presence of the Lord.

*For the Lord gives wisdom;*
*from his mouth come knowledge and understanding.*

PROVERBS 2:6

# WEEKLY

## WEEKLY TRUTH — DAY 07

Scripture is God-breathed and true. When we memorize it, we carry the good news of Jesus with us wherever we go.

As we read the Gospel of Mark, we will memorize a passage about Jesus's presence during His ministry on earth. This week, focus on memorizing verses 43 and 44. Read them out loud several times this week, placing the emphasis on different words each time to help you remember.

*"On the contrary, whoever wants to become great among you will be your servant, and whoever wants to be first among you will be a slave to all. For even the Son of Man did not come to be served, but to serve, and to give his life as a ransom for many."*

*MARK 10:43–45*

THEY WERE EXTREMELY ASTONISHED AND SAID,
"HE HAS DONE EVERYTHING WELL."

# JESUS DOES EVERYTHING WELL

## *DAY 08*

*As you read Mark 7–11, you'll see what Jesus's disciples experienced as they followed Him. Use the space provided on page 74 to make notes on what they witnessed, asked, or were taught.*

### MARK 7

#### THE TRADITIONS OF THE ELDERS

[1] The Pharisees and some of the scribes who had come from Jerusalem gathered around him. [2] They observed that some of his disciples were eating bread with unclean—that is, unwashed—hands. [3] (For the Pharisees and all the Jews do not eat unless they give their hands a ceremonial washing, keeping the tradition of the elders. [4] When they come from the marketplace, they do not eat unless they have washed. And there are many other customs they have received and keep, like the washing of cups, pitchers, kettles, and dining couches.) [5] So the Pharisees and the scribes asked him, "Why don't your disciples live according to the tradition of the elders, instead of eating bread with ceremonially unclean hands?"

[6] He answered them, "Isaiah prophesied correctly about you hypocrites, as it is written:

> This people honors me with their lips,
> but their heart is far from me.
> [7] They worship me in vain,
> teaching as doctrines human commands.

[8] Abandoning the command of God, you hold on to human tradition." [9] He also said to them, "You have a fine way of invalidating God's command in order to set up your tradition! [10] For Moses said: Honor your father and your mother; and Whoever speaks evil of father or mother must be put to death. [11] But you say, 'If anyone tells his father or mother: Whatever benefit you might have received from

me is corban'" (that is, an offering devoted to God), [12] "you no longer let him do anything for his father or mother. [13] You nullify the word of God by your tradition that you have handed down. And you do many other similar things."

[14] Summoning the crowd again, he told them,

## *"Listen to me, all of you, and understand:*

[15] Nothing that goes into a person from outside can defile him but the things that come out of a person are what defile him."

[17] When he went into the house away from the crowd, his disciples asked him about the parable. [18] He said to them, "Are you also as lacking in understanding? Don't you realize that nothing going into a person from the outside can defile him? [19] For it doesn't go into his heart but into the stomach and is eliminated" (thus he declared all foods clean). [20] And he said, "What comes out of a person is what defiles him. [21] For from within, out of people's hearts, come evil thoughts, sexual immoralities, thefts, murders, [22] adulteries, greed, evil actions, deceit, self-indulgence, envy, slander, pride, and foolishness. [23] All these evil things come from within and defile a person."

### A GENTILE MOTHER'S FAITH

[24] He got up and departed from there to the region of Tyre. He entered a house and did not want anyone to know it, but he could not escape notice. [25] Instead, immediately after hearing about him, a woman whose little daughter had an unclean spirit came and fell at his feet. [26] The woman was a Gentile, a Syrophoenician by birth, and she was asking him to cast the demon out of her daughter. [27] He said to her, "Let the children be fed first, because it isn't right to take the children's bread and throw it to the dogs."

[28] But she replied to him, "Lord, even the dogs under the table eat the children's crumbs."

[29] Then he told her, "Because of this reply, you may go. The demon has left your daughter." [30] When she went back to her home, she found her child lying on the bed, and the demon was gone.

### JESUS DOES EVERYTHING WELL

[31] Again, leaving the region of Tyre, he went by way of Sidon to the Sea of Galilee, through the region of the Decapolis. [32] They brought to him a deaf man who had difficulty speaking and begged Jesus to lay his hand on him. [33] So he took him away from the crowd in private. After putting his fingers in the man's ears and spitting, he touched his tongue. [34] Looking up to heaven, he sighed deeply and said

to him, "Ephphatha!" (that is, "Be opened!"). [35] Immediately his ears were opened, his tongue was loosened, and he began to speak clearly. [36] He ordered them to tell no one, but the more he ordered them, the more they proclaimed it.

[37] They were extremely astonished and said, "He has done everything well. He even makes the deaf hear and the mute speak."

## PSALM 51:7–10

[7] Purify me with hyssop, and I will be clean;
wash me, and I will be whiter than snow.
[8] Let me hear joy and gladness;
let the bones you have crushed rejoice.
[9] Turn your face away from my sins
and blot out all my guilt.

*[10] God, create a clean heart for me*
*and renew a steadfast spirit within me.*

## JEREMIAH 17:9–10

THE DECEITFUL HEART

[9] "The heart is more deceitful than anything else,
and incurable—who can understand it?

[10] I, the LORD, examine the mind,
I test the heart
to give to each according to his way,
according to what his actions deserve."

*DAY 09*

# JESUS FEEDS FOUR THOUSAND

## MARK 8

### FEEDING FOUR THOUSAND

[1] In those days there was again a large crowd, and they had nothing to eat. He called the disciples and said to them, [2] "I have compassion on the crowd, because they've already stayed with me three days and have nothing to eat. [3] If I send them home hungry, they will collapse on the way, and some of them have come a long distance."

[4] His disciples answered him, "Where can anyone get enough bread here in this desolate place to feed these people?"

[5] "How many loaves do you have?" he asked them.

"Seven," they said. [6] He commanded the crowd to sit down on the ground.

*Taking the seven loaves, he gave thanks, broke them, and gave them to his disciples*

to set before the people. So they served them to the crowd. [7] They also had a few small fish, and after he had blessed them, he said these were to be served as well. [8] They ate and were satisfied. Then they collected seven large baskets of leftover pieces. [9] About four thousand were there. He dismissed them. [10] And he immediately got into the boat with his disciples and went to the district of Dalmanutha.

### THE LEAVEN OF THE PHARISEES AND HEROD

[11] The Pharisees came and began to argue with him, demanding of him a sign from heaven to test him. [12] Sighing deeply in his spirit, he said, "Why does this generation demand a sign? Truly I tell you, no sign will be given to this generation." [13] Then he left them, got back into the boat, and went to the other side.

[14] The disciples had forgotten to take bread and had only one loaf with them in the boat. [15] Then he gave them strict orders: "Watch out! Beware of the leaven of the Pharisees and the leaven of Herod." [16] They were discussing among themselves that they did not have any bread. [17] Aware of this, he said to them, "Why are you discussing the fact you have no bread? Don't you understand or comprehend? Do you have hardened hearts? [18] Do you have eyes and not see; do you have ears and not hear? And do you not remember? [19] When I broke the five loaves for the five thousand, how many baskets full of leftovers did you collect?"

"Twelve," they told him.

[20] "When I broke the seven loaves for the four thousand, how many baskets full of pieces did you collect?"

"Seven," they said.

[21] And he said to them, "Don't you understand yet?"

HEALING A BLIND MAN

[22] They came to Bethsaida. They brought a blind man to him and begged him to touch him. [23] He took the blind man by the hand and brought him out of the village. Spitting on his eyes and laying his hands on him, he asked him, "Do you see anything?"

[24] He looked up and said, "I see people—they look like trees walking."

[25] Again Jesus placed his hands on the man's eyes. The man looked intently and his sight was restored and he saw everything clearly. [26] Then he sent him home, saying, "Don't even go into the village."

PETER'S CONFESSION OF THE MESSIAH

[27] Jesus went out with his disciples to the villages of Caesarea Philippi. And on the road he asked his disciples, "Who do people say that I am?"

[28] They answered him, "John the Baptist; others, Elijah; still others, one of the prophets."

[29] "But you," he asked them, "who do you say that I am?"

*Peter answered him, "You are the Messiah."*

[30] And he strictly warned them to tell no one about him.

HIS DEATH AND RESURRECTION PREDICTED

[31] Then he began to teach them that it was necessary for the Son of Man to suffer many things and be rejected by the elders, chief priests, and scribes, be killed, and rise after three days. [32] He spoke openly about this. Peter took him aside and began to rebuke him. [33] But turning around and looking at his disciples, he rebuked Peter and said, "Get behind me, Satan! You are not thinking about God's concerns but human concerns."

## TAKE UP YOUR CROSS

[34] Calling the crowd along with his disciples, he said to them,

*"If anyone wants to follow after me, let him deny himself, take up his cross, and follow me.*

[35] For whoever wants to save his life will lose it, but whoever loses his life because of me and the gospel will save it. [36] For what does it benefit someone to gain the whole world and yet lose his life? [37] What can anyone give in exchange for his life? [38] For whoever is ashamed of me and my words in this adulterous and sinful generation, the Son of Man will also be ashamed of him when he comes in the glory of his Father with the holy angels."

## MARK 9:1

Then he said to them, "Truly I tell you, there are some standing here who will not taste death until they see the kingdom of God come in power."

## 2 SAMUEL 7:10–16

[10] "I will designate a place for my people Israel and plant them, so that they may live there and not be disturbed again. Evildoers will not continue to oppress them as they have done [11] ever since the day I ordered judges to be over my people Israel. I will give you rest from all your enemies.

"'The LORD declares to you: The LORD himself will make a house for you. [12] When your time comes and you rest with your ancestors, I will raise up after you your descendant, who will come from your body, and I will establish his kingdom. [13] He is the one who will build a house for my name, and I will establish the throne of his kingdom forever. [14] I will be his father, and he will be my son. When he does wrong, I will discipline him with a rod of men and blows from mortals. [15] But my faithful love will never leave him as it did when I removed it from Saul, whom I removed from before you. [16] Your house and kingdom will endure before me forever, and your throne will be established forever.'"

## DANIEL 7:13–14

[13] I continued watching in the night visions,

and suddenly one like a son of man
was coming with the clouds of heaven.
He approached the Ancient of Days
and was escorted before him.
[14] He was given dominion
and glory and a kingdom,
so that those of every people,
nation, and language
should serve him.
His dominion is an everlasting dominion
that will not pass away,
and his kingdom is one
that will not be destroyed.

# JESUS'S *Miracles* *at a* GLANCE

Throughout His ministry on earth, Jesus performed miracles that showed His compassion. He healed the sick, fed the hungry, calmed stormy seas, and delivered men and women from evil spirits. Here is a look at Jesus's miracles recorded in the Gospels.

OVER

# 9,000

PEOPLE FED

MORE THAN

**39** RECORDED MIRACLES PERFORMED BY JESUS*

5,000+

MT 14:14–21

4,000+

MK 8:1–9

*WHERE DID JESUS PERFORM MIRACLES?*

| NAMED LOCATION | NUMBER OF MIRACLES** |
|---|---|
| CAPERNAUM | 10 |
| THE SEA OF GALILEE | 4 |
| THE DECAPOLIS | 4 |
| JERUSALEM | 3 |
| GALILEE | 2 |
| BETHANY | 1 |
| CANA | 1 |
| NAIN | 1 |
| TYRE & SIDON | 1 |
| CAESAREA | 1 |
| JERICHO | 1 |
| SAMARIA | 1 |
| GETHSEMANE | 1 |

*Numbers differ from scholar to scholar.

**Not all miracles have a named location, while other named locations lie within a wider region. This chart gives a general look at the places where Jesus performed miracles.

"THIS IS MY BELOVED SON; LISTEN TO HIM!"

# JESUS IS TRANSFIGURED

## *DAY 10*

MARK 9:2–50

THE TRANSFIGURATION

[2] After six days Jesus took Peter, James, and John and led them up a high mountain by themselves to be alone. He was transfigured in front of them, [3] and his clothes became dazzling—extremely white as no launderer on earth could whiten them. [4] Elijah appeared to them with Moses, and they were talking with Jesus. [5] Peter said to Jesus, "Rabbi, it's good for us to be here. Let's set up three shelters: one for you, one for Moses, and one for Elijah"— [6] because he did not know what to say, since they were terrified.

[7] A cloud appeared, overshadowing them, and a voice came from the cloud: "This is my beloved Son; listen to him!"

[8] Suddenly, looking around, they no longer saw anyone with them except Jesus.

[9] As they were coming down the mountain, he ordered them to tell no one what they had seen until the Son of Man had risen from the dead. [10] They kept this word to themselves, questioning what "rising from the dead" meant.

[11] Then they asked him, "Why do the scribes say that Elijah must come first?"

[12] "Elijah does come first and restores all things," he replied. "Why then is it written that the Son of Man must suffer many things and be treated with contempt? [13] But I tell you that Elijah has come, and they did whatever they pleased to him, just as it is written about him."

### THE POWER OF FAITH OVER A DEMON

[14] When they came to the disciples, they saw a large crowd around them and scribes disputing with them. [15] When the whole crowd saw him, they were amazed and ran to greet him. [16] He asked them, "What are you arguing with them about?"

[17] Someone from the crowd answered him, "Teacher, I brought my son to you. He has a spirit that makes him unable to speak. [18] Whenever it seizes him, it throws him down, and he foams at the mouth, grinds his teeth, and becomes rigid. I asked your disciples to drive it out, but they couldn't."

[19] He replied to them, "You unbelieving generation, how long will I be with you? How long must I put up with you? Bring him to me." [20] So they brought the boy to him. When the spirit saw him, it immediately threw the boy into convulsions. He fell to the ground and rolled around, foaming at the mouth. [21] "How long has this been happening to him?" Jesus asked his father.

"From childhood," he said. [22] "And many times it has thrown him into fire or water to destroy him. But if you can do anything, have compassion on us and help us."

[23] Jesus said to him, "'If you can'? Everything is possible for the one who believes."

[24] Immediately the father of the boy cried out, "I do believe; help my unbelief!"

[25] When Jesus saw that a crowd was quickly gathering, he rebuked the unclean spirit, saying to it, "You mute and deaf spirit, I command you: Come out of him and never enter him again."

[26] Then it came out, shrieking and throwing him into terrible convulsions. The boy became like a corpse, so that many said, "He's dead." [27] But Jesus, taking him by the hand, raised him, and he stood up.

[28] After he had gone into the house, his disciples asked him privately, "Why couldn't we drive it out?"

[29] And he told them, "This kind can come out by nothing but prayer."

### THE SECOND PREDICTION OF HIS DEATH

[30] Then they left that place and made their way through Galilee, but he did not want anyone to know it. [31] For he was teaching his disciples and telling them, "The Son of Man is going to be betrayed into the hands of men. They will kill him, and after he is killed, he will rise three days later." [32] But they did not understand this statement, and they were afraid to ask him.

### WHO IS THE GREATEST?

[33] They came to Capernaum. When he was in the house, he asked them, "What were you arguing about on the way?" [34] But they were silent, because on the way they had been arguing with one another about who was the greatest. [35] Sitting down, he called the Twelve and said to them, "If anyone wants to be first, he must be last and servant of all." [36] He took a child, had him stand among them, and taking him in his arms, he said to them, [37] "Whoever welcomes one little child such as this in my name welcomes me. And whoever welcomes me does not welcome me, but him who sent me."

### IN HIS NAME

[38] John said to him, "Teacher, we saw someone driving out demons in your name, and we tried to stop him because he wasn't following us."

[39] "Don't stop him," said Jesus, "because there is no one who will perform a miracle in my name who can soon afterward speak evil of me. [40] For whoever is not against us is for us. [41] And whoever gives you a cup of water to drink in my name, because you belong to Christ—truly I tell you, he will never lose his reward.

### WARNINGS FROM JESUS

[42] "But whoever causes one of these little ones who believe in me to fall away—it would be better for him if a heavy millstone were hung around his neck and he were thrown into the sea.

[43] "And if your hand causes you to fall away, cut it off. It is better for you to enter life maimed than to have two hands and go to hell, the unquenchable fire. [45] And if your foot causes you to fall away, cut it off. It is better for you to enter life lame than to have two feet and be thrown into hell. [47] And if your eye causes you to fall away, gouge it out. It is better for you to enter the kingdom of God with one eye than to have two eyes and be thrown into hell, [48] where their worm does not die, and the fire is not quenched. [49] For everyone will be salted with fire. [50] Salt is good, but if the salt should lose its flavor, how can you season it? Have salt among yourselves, and be at peace with one another."

## EZEKIEL 43:24

"You are to present them before the LORD; the priests will throw salt on them and sacrifice them as a burnt offering to the LORD."

## PHILIPPIANS 1:15–19

[15] To be sure, some preach Christ out of envy and rivalry, but others out of good will. [16] These preach out of love, knowing that I am appointed for the defense of the gospel; [17] the others proclaim Christ out of selfish ambition, not sincerely, thinking that they will cause me trouble in my imprisonment. [18] What does it matter? Only that in every way, whether from false motives or true, Christ is proclaimed, and in this I rejoice. Yes, and I will continue to rejoice [19] because I know this will lead to my salvation through your prayers and help from the Spirit of Jesus Christ.

DAY 11

# POSSESSIONS AND THE KINGDOM

## MARK 10

### THE QUESTION OF DIVORCE

[1] He set out from there and went to the region of Judea and across the Jordan. Then crowds converged on him again, and as was his custom he taught them again.

[2] Some Pharisees came to test him, asking, "Is it lawful for a man to divorce his wife?"

[3] He replied to them, "What did Moses command you?"

[4] They said, "Moses permitted us to write divorce papers and send her away."

[5] But Jesus told them, "He wrote this command for you because of the hardness of your hearts. [6] But from the beginning of creation God made them male and female. [7] For this reason a man will leave his father and mother [8] and the two will become one flesh. So they are no longer two, but one flesh. [9] Therefore what God has joined together, let no one separate."

[10] When they were in the house again, the disciples questioned him about this matter. [11] He said to them, "Whoever divorces his wife and marries another commits adultery against her. [12] Also, if she divorces her husband and marries another, she commits adultery."

### BLESSING THE CHILDREN

[13] People were bringing little children to him in order that he might touch them, but the disciples rebuked them. [14] When Jesus saw it, he was indignant and said to them, "Let the little children come to me. Don't stop them, because the kingdom of God belongs to such as these. [15] Truly I tell you,

*whoever does not receive the kingdom of God like a little child will never enter it."*

[16] After taking them in his arms, he laid his hands on them and blessed them.

### THE RICH YOUNG RULER

[17] As he was setting out on a journey, a man ran up, knelt down before him, and asked him, "Good teacher, what must I do to inherit eternal life?"

[18] "Why do you call me good?" Jesus asked him. "No one is good except God alone. [19] You know the commandments: Do not murder; do not commit adultery; do not steal; do not bear false witness; do not defraud; honor your father and mother."

[20] He said to him, "Teacher, I have kept all these from my youth."

[21] Looking at him, Jesus loved him and said to him, "You lack one thing: Go, sell all you have and give to the poor, and you will have treasure in heaven. Then come, follow me." [22] But he was dismayed by this demand, and he went away grieving, because he had many possessions.

### POSSESSIONS AND THE KINGDOM

[23] Jesus looked around and said to his disciples, "How hard it is for those who have wealth to enter the kingdom of God!"

[24] The disciples were astonished at his words. Again Jesus said to them, "Children, how hard it is to enter the kingdom of God! [25] It is easier for a camel to go through the eye of a needle than for a rich person to enter the kingdom of God."

[26] They were even more astonished, saying to one another, "Then who can be saved?"

[27] Looking at them, Jesus said,

*"With man it is impossible, but not with God, because all things are possible with God."*

[28] Peter began to tell him, "Look, we have left everything and followed you."

[29] "Truly I tell you," Jesus said, "there is no one who has left house or brothers or sisters or mother or father or children or fields for my sake and for the sake of the gospel, [30] who will not receive a hundred times more, now at this time — houses, brothers and sisters, mothers and children, and fields, with persecutions —and eternal life in the age to come. [31] But many who are first will be last, and the last first."

### THE THIRD PREDICTION OF HIS DEATH

[32] They were on the road, going up to Jerusalem, and Jesus was walking ahead of them. The disciples were astonished, but those who followed him were afraid. Taking the Twelve aside again, he began to tell them the things that would happen to him. [33] "See, we are going up to Jerusalem. The Son of Man will be handed over to the chief priests and the scribes, and they will condemn him to death. Then they will hand him over to the Gentiles, [34] and they will mock him, spit on him, flog him, and kill him, and he will rise after three days."

SUFFERING AND SERVICE

[35] James and John, the sons of Zebedee, approached him and said, "Teacher, we want you to do whatever we ask you."

[36] "What do you want me to do for you?" he asked them.

[37] They answered him, "Allow us to sit at your right and at your left in your glory."

[38] Jesus said to them, "You don't know what you're asking. Are you able to drink the cup I drink or to be baptized with the baptism I am baptized with?"

[39] "We are able," they told him.

Jesus said to them, "You will drink the cup I drink, and you will be baptized with the baptism I am baptized with. [40] But to sit at my right or left is not mine to give; instead, it is for those for whom it has been prepared."

[41] When the ten disciples heard this, they began to be indignant with James and John. [42] Jesus called them over and said to them, "You know that those who are regarded as rulers of the Gentiles lord it over them, and those in high positions act as tyrants over them. [43] But it is not so among you.

*On the contrary, whoever wants to become great among you will be your servant, [44] and whoever wants to be first among you will be a slave to all.*

[45] For even the Son of Man did not come to be served, but to serve, and to give his life as a ransom for many."

A BLIND MAN HEALED

[46] They came to Jericho. And as he was leaving Jericho with his disciples and a large crowd, Bartimaeus (the son of Timaeus), a blind beggar, was sitting by the road. [47] When he heard that it was Jesus of Nazareth, he began to cry out, "Jesus, Son of David, have mercy on me!" [48] Many warned him to keep quiet, but he was crying out all the more, "Have mercy on me, Son of David!"

[49] Jesus stopped and said, "Call him."

So they called the blind man and said to him, "Have courage! Get up; he's calling for you." [50] He threw off his coat, jumped up, and came to Jesus.

[51] Then Jesus answered him, "What do you want me to do for you?"

"*Rabboni*," the blind man said to him, "I want to see."

[52] Jesus said to him, "Go, your faith has saved you." Immediately he could see and began to follow Jesus on the road.

ISAIAH 51:17

"Wake yourself, wake yourself up!
Stand up, Jerusalem,
you who have drunk the cup of his fury
from the LORD's hand;
you who have drunk the goblet to the dregs—
the cup that causes people to stagger."

1 PETER 4:13

*Instead, rejoice as you share in the sufferings of Christ, so that you may also rejoice with great joy when his glory is revealed.*

# THE SON *of* GOD

Starting with the author's first statement, the Gospel of Mark presents Jesus Christ as the Son of God. These confessions come from a variety of witnesses who testify to the divine nature of Christ. As you read this collection of statements, consider who you believe Jesus to be.

## MARK

*The beginning of the gospel of Jesus Christ, the Son of God.* ***1:1***

## GOD *the* FATHER

*"You are my beloved Son; with you I am well-pleased."* ***1:11***

*"This is my beloved Son; listen to him!"* ***9:7***

## THE CENTURION

*Truly this man was the Son of God!* ***15:39***

## PETER

*You are the Messiah.* ***8:29***

*"For even the Son of Man did not come to be served, but to serve, and to give his life as a ransom for many."* **10:45**

*"But so that you may know that the Son of Man has authority on earth to forgive sins"—he told the paralytic—"I tell you: get up, take your mat, and go home."* **2:10–11**

# JESUS

*"The Son of Man is going to be betrayed into the hands of men. They will kill him, and after he is killed, he will rise three days later."* **9:31**

*"For the Son of Man will go just as it is written about him, but woe to that man by whom the Son of Man is betrayed!"* **14:21**

*"For whoever is ashamed of me and my words in this adulterous and sinful generation, the Son of Man will also be ashamed of him when he comes in the glory of his Father..."* **8:38**

*"The Son of Man is Lord even of the Sabbath."* **2:28**

*Again the high priest questioned him, "Are you the Messiah, the Son of the Blessed One?" "I am," said Jesus, "and you will see the Son of Man seated at the right hand of Power and coming with the clouds of heaven."* **14:61–62**

# UNCLEAN SPIRITS

*What do you have to do with us, Jesus of Nazareth? Have you come to destroy us? I know who you are—the Holy One of God!* **1:24**

*You are the Son of God!* **3:11**

*What do you have to do with me, Jesus, Son of the Most High God? I beg you before God, don't torment me!* **5:7**

# JESUS RIDES INTO JERUSALEM

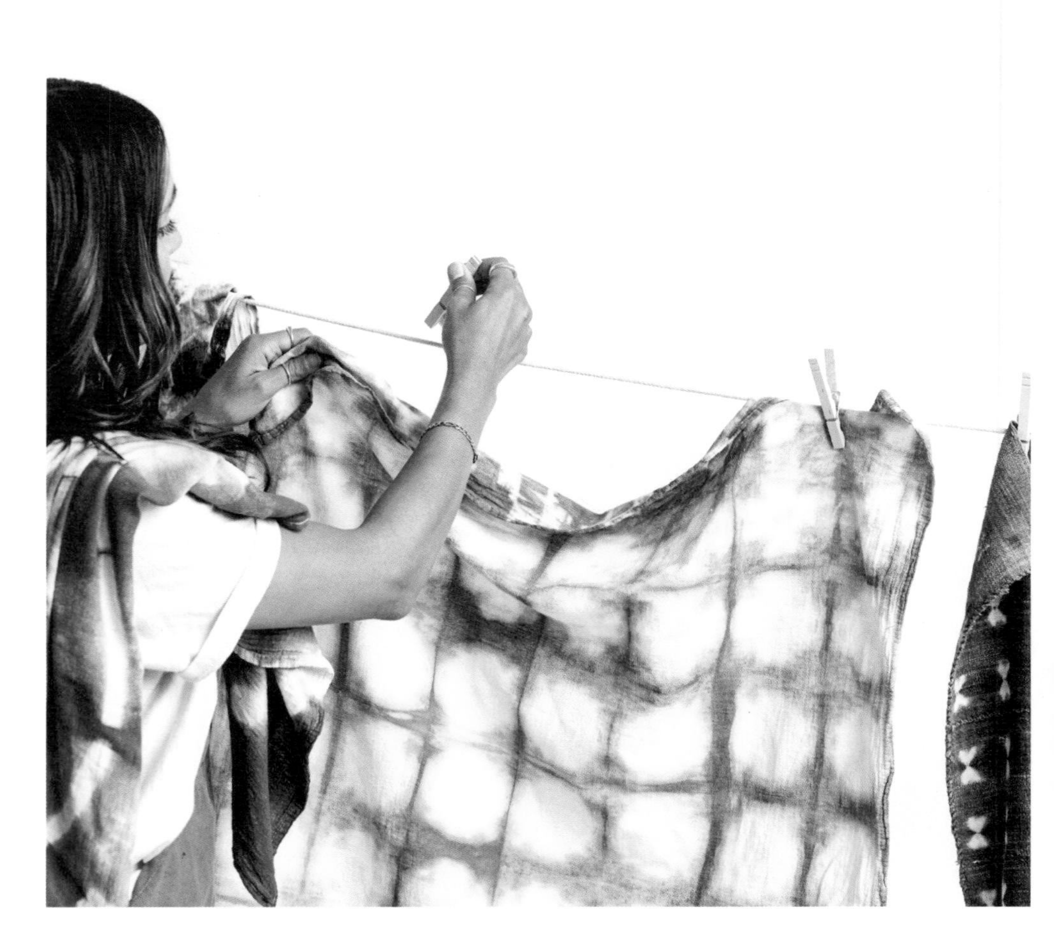

*DAY 12*

## MARK 11

### THE TRIUMPHAL ENTRY

[1] When they approached Jerusalem, at Bethphage and Bethany near the Mount of Olives, he sent two of his disciples [2] and told them, "Go into the village ahead of you. As soon as you enter it, you will find a colt tied there, on which no one has ever sat. Untie it and bring it. [3] If anyone says to you, 'Why are you doing this?' say, 'The Lord needs it and will send it back here right away.'"

[4] So they went and found a colt outside in the street, tied by a door. They untied it, [5] and some of those standing there said to them, "What are you doing, untying the colt?" [6] They answered them just as Jesus had said; so they let them go.

[7] They brought the colt to Jesus and threw their clothes on it, and he sat on it. [8] Many people spread their clothes on the road, and others spread leafy branches cut from the fields. [9] Those who went ahead and those who followed shouted:

> *Hosanna!*
> Blessed is he who comes
> in the name of the Lord!
> [10] Blessed is the coming kingdom
> of our father David!
> *Hosanna* in the highest heaven!

[11] He went into Jerusalem and into the temple. After looking around at everything, since it was already late, he went out to Bethany with the Twelve.

### THE BARREN FIG TREE IS CURSED

[12] The next day when they went out from Bethany, he was hungry. [13] Seeing in the distance a fig tree with leaves, he went to find out if there was anything on it. When he came to it, he found nothing but leaves; for it was not the season for figs. [14] He said to it, "May no one ever eat fruit from you again!" And his disciples heard it.

### CLEANSING THE TEMPLE

[15] They came to Jerusalem, and he went into the temple and began to throw out those buying and selling. He overturned the tables of the money changers and the chairs of those selling doves, [16] and would not permit anyone to carry goods through the temple. [17] He was teaching them:

*"Is it not written, My house will be called a house of prayer for all nations?*

But you have made it a den of thieves!"

## MARKAN SANDWICH

*MARK 11:12–25*

**Opens with**

Jesus cursing a barren fig tree for its failure to provide fruit.

**Shifts to**

Jesus clearing the money changers out of the temple.

**Returns to**

the cursed fig tree, withered and dead.

[18] The chief priests and the scribes heard it and started looking for a way to kill him. For they were afraid of him, because the whole crowd was astonished by his teaching.

[19] Whenever evening came, they would go out of the city.

### THE BARREN FIG TREE IS WITHERED

[20] Early in the morning, as they were passing by, they saw the fig tree withered from the roots up. [21] Then Peter remembered and said to him, "Rabbi, look! The fig tree that you cursed has withered."

[22] Jesus replied to them, "Have faith in God. [23] Truly I tell you, if anyone says to this mountain, 'Be lifted up and thrown into the sea,' and does not doubt in his heart, but believes that what he says will happen, it will be done for him. [24] Therefore I tell you, everything you pray and ask for—believe that you have received it and it will be yours. [25] And whenever you stand praying, if you have anything against anyone, forgive him, so that your Father in heaven will also forgive you your wrongdoing."

### THE AUTHORITY OF JESUS CHALLENGED

[27] They came again to Jerusalem. As he was walking in the temple, the chief priests, the scribes, and the elders came [28] and asked him, "By what authority are you doing these things? Who gave you this authority to do these things?"

[29] Jesus said to them, "I will ask you one question; then answer me, and I will tell you by what authority I do these things. [30] Was John's baptism from heaven or of human origin? Answer me."

[31] They discussed it among themselves: "If we say, 'From heaven,' he will say, 'Then why didn't you believe him?' [32] But if we say, 'Of human origin'"—they were afraid of the crowd, because everyone thought that John was truly a prophet. [33] So they answered Jesus, "We don't know."

And Jesus said to them, "Neither will I tell you by what authority I do these things."

PSALM 118:25–26

[25] LORD, save us!
LORD, please grant us success!
[26] He who comes in the name
of the LORD is blessed.
From the house of the LORD we bless you.

ZECHARIAH 9:9

*Rejoice greatly, Daughter Zion!*
*Shout in triumph, Daughter Jerusalem!*
*Look, your King is coming to you;*
*he is righteous and victorious,*
*humble and riding on a donkey,*
*on a colt, the foal of a donkey.*

# WEEK *2*
## *Reflection*

As people began to follow Jesus, they witnessed His miracles, asked Him questions, and learned from His teaching. Look back over this week's reading to make notes on what followers of Jesus witnessed, asked, or were taught in each of the stories listed below.

CONFRONTATION *with the* ELDERS — *DAY 8*

SYROPHOENICIAN WOMAN — *DAY 8*

THE DEAF MAN — *DAY 8*

FEEDING *of the* FOUR THOUSAND — *DAY 9*

THE TRANSFIGURATION — *DAY 10*

CONVERSATIONS *in* CAPERNAUM — *DAY 10*

DISCUSSION *with the* PHARISEES — *DAY 11*

BLESSING *the* CHILDREN — *DAY 11*

CONVERSATIONS *on the* JOURNEY — *DAY 11*

MARK 8:34

"IF ANYONE WANTS TO FOLLOW AFTER ME, LET HIM DENY HIMSELF, TAKE UP HIS CROSS, AND FOLLOW ME."

Reflect on what it has looked like for you to follow Jesus. In the journaling space below, write about your experience. What have you seen as you've followed Him? What have you learned about who He is?

GR

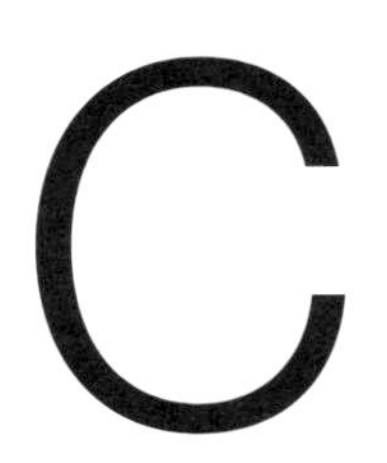

E

Take this day to catch up on your reading, pray, and rest in the presence of the Lord.

*He who comes in the name*
*of the Lord is blessed.*
*From the house of the Lord we bless you.*

*PSALM 118:26*

# WE EK

# LY

## WEEKLY TRUTH — DAY 14

Scripture is God-breathed and true. When we memorize it, we carry the good news of Jesus with us wherever we go.

This week, we will memorize the last verse in Mark 10:43–45. Write verse 45 a few times in the space provided. Then read the full passage aloud, meditating on these words from Jesus.

*"On the contrary, whoever wants to become great among you will be your servant, and whoever wants to be first among you will be a slave to all. For even the Son of Man did not come to be served, but to serve, and to give his life as a ransom for many."*

# *MARK 10:43–45*

"LOVE THE LORD YOUR GOD WITH ALL YOUR HEART, WITH ALL YOUR SOUL, WITH ALL YOUR MIND, AND WITH ALL YOUR STRENGTH."

# JESUS GIVES THE GREATEST COMMANDMENT

## *DAY 15*

*As you read Mark 12–16, you'll see many different people and groups encountering Jesus. Notice how they respond to Him. At the end of this week on page 114, you'll find space to reflect on their encounters as well as your own.*

### MARK 12

#### THE PARABLE OF THE VINEYARD OWNER

[1] He began to speak to them in parables: "A man planted a vineyard, put a fence around it, dug out a pit for a winepress, and built a watchtower. Then he leased it to tenant farmers and went away. [2] At harvest time he sent a servant to the farmers to collect some of the fruit of the vineyard from them. [3] But they took him, beat him, and sent him away empty-handed. [4] Again he sent another servant to them, and they hit him on the head and treated him shamefully. [5] Then he sent another, and they killed that one. He also sent many others; some they beat, and others they killed. [6] He still had one to send, a beloved son. Finally he sent him to them, saying, 'They will respect my son.' [7] But those tenant farmers said to one another, 'This is the heir. Come, let's kill him, and the inheritance will be ours.' [8] So they seized him, killed him, and threw him out of the vineyard. [9] What then will the owner of the vineyard do? He will come and kill the farmers and give the vineyard to others. [10] Haven't you read this Scripture:

The stone that the builders rejected
has become the cornerstone.
[11] This came about from the Lord
and is wonderful in our eyes?"

[12] They were looking for a way to arrest him but feared the crowd because they knew he had spoken this parable against them. So they left him and went away.

### GOD AND CAESAR

[13] Then they sent some of the Pharisees and the Herodians to Jesus to trap him in his words. [14] When they came, they said to him, "Teacher, we know you are truthful and don't care what anyone thinks, nor do you show partiality but teach the way of God truthfully. Is it lawful to pay taxes to Caesar or not? Should we pay or shouldn't we?"

[15] But knowing their hypocrisy, he said to them, "Why are you testing me? Bring me a denarius to look at." [16] They brought a coin. "Whose image and inscription is this?" he asked them.

"Caesar's," they replied.

[17] Jesus told them, "Give to Caesar the things that are Caesar's, and to God the things that are God's." And they were utterly amazed at him.

### THE SADDUCEES AND THE RESURRECTION

[18] Sadducees, who say there is no resurrection, came to him and questioned him: [19] "Teacher, Moses wrote for us that if a man's brother dies, leaving a wife behind but no child, that man should take the wife and raise up offspring for his brother. [20] There were seven brothers. The first married a woman, and dying, left no offspring. [21] The second also took her, and he died, leaving no offspring. And the third likewise. [22] None of the seven left offspring. Last of all, the woman died too. [23] In the resurrection, when they rise, whose wife will she be, since the seven had married her?"

[24] Jesus spoke to them, "Isn't this the reason why you're mistaken: you don't know the Scriptures or the power of God? [25] For when they rise from the dead, they neither marry nor are given in marriage but are like angels in heaven. [26] And as for the dead being raised—haven't you read in the book of Moses, in the passage about the burning bush, how God said to him: I am the God of Abraham and the God of Isaac and the God of Jacob? [27] He is not the God of the dead but of the living. You are badly mistaken."

### THE PRIMARY COMMANDS

[28] One of the scribes approached. When he heard them debating and saw that Jesus answered them well, he asked him, "Which command is the most important of all?"

[29] Jesus answered, "The most important is Listen, Israel! The Lord our God, the Lord is one. [30] Love the Lord your God with all your heart, with all your soul, with all your mind, and with all your strength. [31] The second is, Love your neighbor as yourself. There is no other command greater than these."

[32] Then the scribe said to him, "You are right, teacher. You have correctly said that he is one, and there is no one else except him. [33] And to love him with all your heart, with all your understanding, and with all your strength, and to love your neighbor as yourself, is far more important than all the burnt offerings and sacrifices."

[34] When Jesus saw that he answered wisely, he said to him, "You are not far from the kingdom of God." And no one dared to question him any longer.

### THE QUESTION ABOUT THE MESSIAH

[35] While Jesus was teaching in the temple, he asked, "How can the scribes say that the Messiah is the son of David? [36] David himself says by the Holy Spirit:

The Lord declared to my Lord,
'Sit at my right hand
until I put your enemies under your feet.'

[37] David himself calls him 'Lord.' How, then, can he be his son?" And the large crowd was listening to him with delight.

### WARNING AGAINST THE SCRIBES

[38] He also said in his teaching, "Beware of the scribes, who want to go around in long robes and who want greetings in the marketplaces, [39] the best seats in the synagogues, and the places of honor at banquets. [40] They devour widows' houses and say long prayers just for show. These will receive harsher judgment."

THE WIDOW'S GIFT

[41] Sitting across from the temple treasury, he watched how the crowd dropped money into the treasury. Many rich people were putting in large sums. [42] Then a poor widow came and dropped in two tiny coins worth very little. [43] Summoning his disciples, he said to them, "Truly I tell you, this poor widow has put more into the treasury than all the others. [44] For they all gave out of their surplus, but she out of her poverty has put in everything she had —all she had to live on."

## JOSHUA 22:1–5

EASTERN TRIBES RETURN HOME

[1] Joshua summoned the Reubenites, Gadites, and half the tribe of Manasseh [2] and told them, "You have done everything Moses the LORD's servant commanded you and have obeyed me in everything I commanded you. [3] You have not deserted your brothers even once this whole time but have carried out the requirement of the command of the LORD your God. [4] Now that he has given your brothers rest, just as he promised them, return to your homes in your own land that Moses the LORD's servant gave you across the Jordan. [5] Only carefully obey the command and instruction that Moses the LORD's servant gave you: to love the LORD your God, walk in all his ways, keep his commands, be loyal to him, and serve him with all your heart and all your soul."

## 1 PETER 2:4–8

[4] As you come to him, a living stone—rejected by people but chosen and honored by God— [5] you yourselves, as living stones, a spiritual house, are being built to be a holy priesthood to offer spiritual sacrifices acceptable to God through Jesus Christ. [6] For it stands in Scripture:

See, I lay a stone in Zion,
a chosen and honored cornerstone,
and the one who believes in him
will never be put to shame.

[7] So honor will come to you who believe; but for the unbelieving,

The stone that the builders rejected—
this one has become the cornerstone,

[8] and

A stone to stumble over,
and a rock to trip over.

They stumble because they disobey the word; they were destined for this.

*DAY 16*

# JESUS PREDICTS HIS RETURN

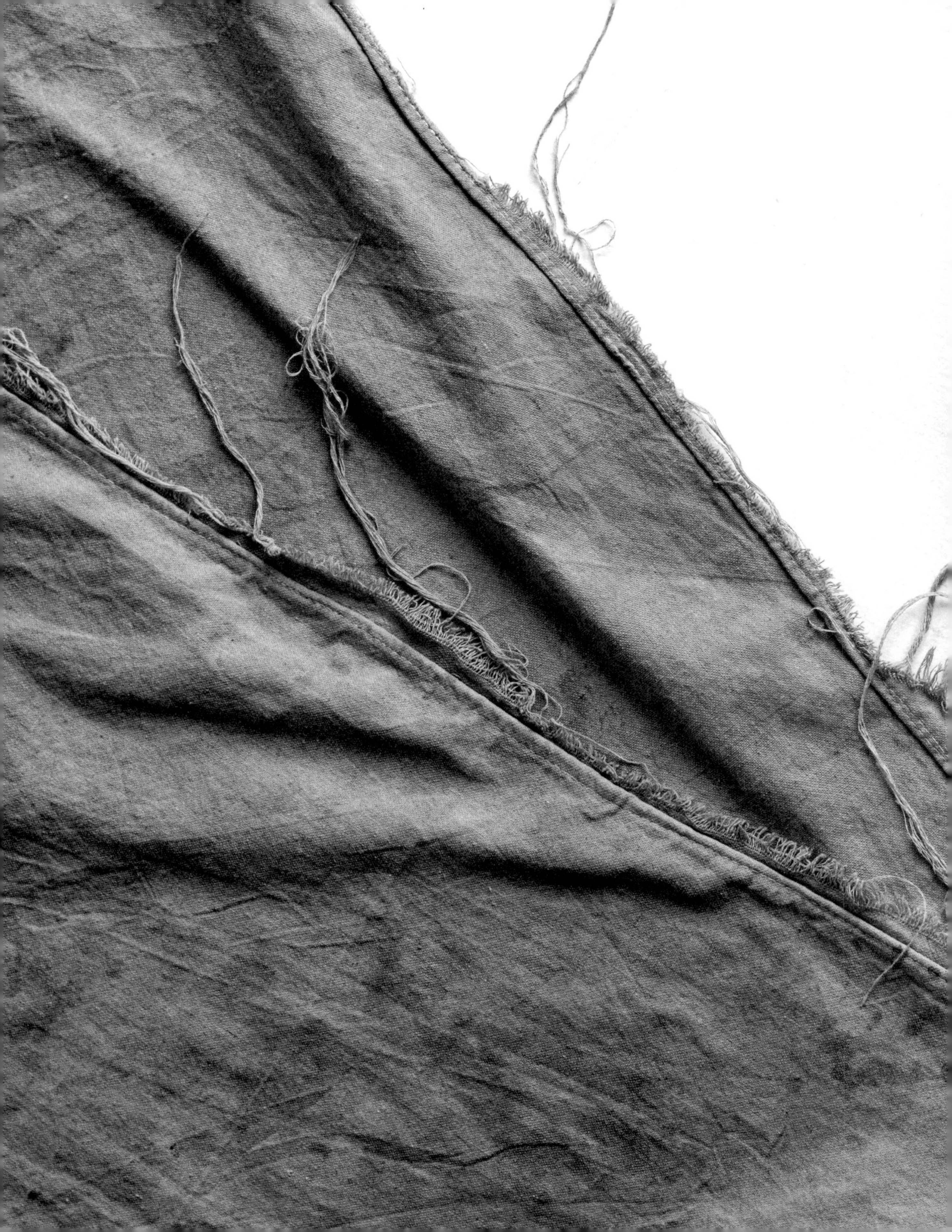

## MARK 13

### DESTRUCTION OF THE TEMPLE PREDICTED

[1] As he was going out of the temple, one of his disciples said to him, "Teacher, look! What massive stones! What impressive buildings!"

[2] Jesus said to him, "Do you see these great buildings? Not one stone will be left upon another—all will be thrown down."

### SIGNS OF THE END OF THE AGE

[3] While he was sitting on the Mount of Olives across from the temple, Peter, James, John, and Andrew asked him privately, [4] "Tell us, when will these things happen? And what will be the sign when all these things are about to be accomplished?"

[5] Jesus told them, "Watch out that no one deceives you. [6] Many will come in my name, saying, 'I am he,' and they will deceive many. [7] When you hear of wars and rumors of wars, don't be alarmed; these things must take place, but it is not yet the end. [8] For nation will rise up against nation, and kingdom against kingdom. There will be earthquakes in various places, and famines. These are the beginning of birth pains.

### PERSECUTIONS PREDICTED

[9] "But you, be on your guard! They will hand you over to local courts, and you will be flogged in the synagogues. You will stand before governors and kings because of me, as a witness to them. [10] And it is necessary that the gospel be preached to all nations. [11] So when they arrest you and hand you over, don't worry beforehand what you will say, but say whatever is given to you at that time, for it isn't you speaking, but the Holy Spirit.

[12] "Brother will betray brother to death, and a father his child. Children will rise up against parents and have them put to death. [13] You will be hated by everyone because of my name, but the one who endures to the end will be saved.

### THE GREAT TRIBULATION

[14] "When you see the abomination of desolation standing where it should not be" (let the reader understand), "then those in Judea must flee to the mountains. [15] A man on the housetop must not come down or go in to get anything out of his house, [16] and a man in the field must not go back to get his coat. [17] Woe to pregnant women and nursing mothers in those days!

[18] "Pray it won't happen in winter. [19] For those will be days of tribulation, the kind that hasn't been from the beginning of creation until now and never will be again. [20] If the Lord had not cut those days short, no one would be saved. But he cut those days short for the sake of the elect, whom he chose.

[21] "Then if anyone tells you, 'See, here is the Messiah! See, there!' do not believe it. [22] For false messiahs and false prophets will arise and will perform signs and wonders to lead astray, if possible, the elect. [23] And you must watch! I have told you everything in advance.

### THE COMING OF THE SON OF MAN

[24] "But in those days, after that tribulation: The sun will be darkened, and the moon will not shed its light; [25] the stars will be falling from the sky, and the powers in the heavens will be shaken. [26] Then they will see the Son of Man coming in clouds with great power and glory. [27] He will send out the angels and gather his elect from the four winds, from the ends of the earth to the ends of heaven.

### THE PARABLE OF THE FIG TREE

[28] "Learn this lesson from the fig tree: As soon as its branch becomes tender and sprouts leaves, you know that summer is near. [29] In the same way, when you see these things happening, recognize that he is near—at the door.

[30] "Truly I tell you, this generation will certainly not pass away until all these things take place. [31] Heaven and earth will pass away, but my words will never pass away.

### NO ONE KNOWS THE DAY OR HOUR

[32] "Now concerning that day or hour no one knows—neither the angels in heaven nor the Son —but only the Father.

[33] "Watch! Be alert! For you don't know when the time is coming.

[34] "It is like a man on a journey, who left his house, gave authority to his servants, gave each one his work, and commanded the doorkeeper to be alert. [35] Therefore be alert, since you don't know when the master of the house is coming—whether in the evening or at midnight or at the crowing of the rooster or early in the morning. [36] Otherwise, when he comes suddenly he might find you sleeping. [37] And what I say to you, I say to everyone: Be alert!"

## ISAIAH 51:6

Look up to the heavens,
and look at the earth beneath;
for the heavens will vanish like smoke,
the earth will wear out like a garment,
and its inhabitants will die like gnats.
But my salvation will last forever,
and my righteousness will never be shattered.

## JEREMIAH 31:35–37

[35] "This is what the LORD says:

The one who gives the sun for light by day,
the fixed order of moon and stars for light by night,
who stirs up the sea and makes its waves roar—
the LORD of Armies is his name:
[36] If this fixed order departs from before me—
this is the LORD's declaration—
only then will Israel's descendants cease
to be a nation before me forever.

[37] "This is what the LORD says:

Only if the heavens above can be measured
and the foundations of the earth below explored,
will I reject all of Israel's descendants
because of all they have done—
this is the LORD's declaration."

MAP

# HOLY WEEK *in* JERUSALEM

*1* SUNDAY
Jesus descends from Bethany and enters the temple precincts.

*2* SUNDAY NIGHT
Jesus returns to Bethany to lodge with friends.

*3* MONDAY
Jesus cleanses the temple.

*4* TUESDAY
Jesus teaches His disciples about the end times on the Mount of Olives.

*5* THURSDAY
Jesus shares the Passover meal with His disciples.

*6* THURSDAY EVENING
Jesus retires to Gethsemane.

*7* THURSDAY NIGHT
Jesus is arrested.

*8* THURSDAY/FRIDAY
Jesus is taken to the house of Caiaphas for a preliminary hearing.

*9* FRIDAY DAYBREAK
Jesus appears before the Sanhedrin.

*10* FRIDAY DAYBREAK
Jesus appears before Pilate.

*11* FRIDAY MORNING
Jesus appears before Herod Antipas.

*12* FRIDAY MORNING
Jesus appears again before Pilate.

*13* FRIDAY MORNING
Jesus is crucified.

*14* FRIDAY EVENING
Jesus is buried.

*15* SUNDAY
Jesus is resurrected and leaves the tomb.

# JESUS'S *final* HOURS

The ministry of Jesus wasn't hindered by the threat of His crucifixion. Rather, it continued through the events leading up to His death and through His crucifixion and glorious resurrection. Here is an in-depth look at these transformative hours.

## THURSDAY

### 6–9 P.M.

*6 p.m.*

Jesus celebrates Passover with His disciples.

*7 p.m.*

Jesus washes His disciples' feet.

*9 p.m.*

Jesus prays for His disciples, for all believers, and for Himself.

## FRIDAY

### MIDNIGHT–4 A.M.

*Midnight*

Jesus and His disciples pray in the garden of Gethsemane.

*3 a.m.*

Jesus is arrested.

*4 a.m.*

Jesus appears before Annas.

Peter denies Jesus.

### 6–9 A.M.

*6 a.m.*

Jesus stands trial before Pilate and Herod.

*7 a.m.*

Jesus is sentenced to death.

*8 a.m.*

Jesus is led away to Calvary.

*9 a.m.*

Jesus is crucified.

### 10 A.M.–NOON

*10 a.m.*

Jesus is mocked while on the cross.

*Noon*

Darkness covers the land.

### 3–6 P.M.

*3 p.m.*

Jesus gives up His Spirit.

The temple curtain is torn.

The earth shakes.

Many dead saints rise, and they appear in Jerusalem after Jesus's resurrection.

*4 p.m.*

Jesus is taken down from the cross.

*5 p.m.*

Jesus is buried.

*6 p.m.*

The Sabbath begins.

*Times are approximate and site locations are estimates based on archaeological evidence, biblical scholarship, and the location of the city walls during the time of Christ.*

*DAY 17*

# PLOTTING AND PREPARATION

# MARKAN SANDWICH

*MARK 14:1–11*

**Opens with**

the chief priests and scribes looking for a way to condemn Jesus.

**Shifts to**

a woman anointing Jesus's feet with oil.

**Returns to**

Judas Iscariot scheming with the chief priests to betray Jesus.

## MARK 14:1–16

### THE PLOT TO KILL JESUS

[1] It was two days before the Passover and the Festival of Unleavened Bread. The chief priests and the scribes were looking for a cunning way to arrest Jesus and kill him. [2] "Not during the festival," they said, "so that there won't be a riot among the people."

### THE ANOINTING AT BETHANY

[3] While he was in Bethany at the house of Simon the leper, as he was reclining at the table, a woman came with an alabaster jar of very expensive perfume of pure nard. She broke the jar and poured it on his head. [4] But some were expressing indignation to one another: "Why has this perfume been wasted? [5] For this perfume might have been sold for more than three hundred denarii and given to the poor." And they began to scold her.

[6] Jesus replied, "Leave her alone. Why are you bothering her? She has done a noble thing for me. [7] You always have the poor with you, and you can do what is good for them whenever you want, but you do not always have me. [8] She has done what she could; she has anointed my body in advance for burial.

*[9] Truly I tell you, wherever the gospel is proclaimed in the whole world, what she has done will also be told in memory of her."*

[10] Then Judas Iscariot, one of the Twelve, went to the chief priests to betray Jesus to them. [11] And when they heard this, they were glad and promised to give him money. So he started looking for a good opportunity to betray him.

### PREPARATION FOR PASSOVER

[12] On the first day of Unleavened Bread, when they sacrifice the Passover lamb, his disciples asked him, "Where do you want us to go and prepare the Passover so that you may eat it?"

[13] So he sent two of his disciples and told them, "Go into the city, and a man carrying a jar of water will meet you. Follow him. [14] Wherever he enters, tell the owner of the house, 'The Teacher says, "Where is my guest room where I may eat the Passover with my disciples?"' [15] He will show you a large room upstairs, furnished and ready. Make the preparations for us there." [16] So the disciples went out, entered the city, and found it just as he had told them, and they prepared the Passover.

## EXODUS 12:21–28

[21] Then Moses summoned all the elders of Israel and said to them, "Go, select an animal from the flock according to your families, and slaughter the Passover animal. [22] Take a cluster of hyssop, dip it in the blood that is in the basin, and brush the lintel and the two doorposts with some of the blood in the basin. None of you may go out the door of his house until morning. [23] When the LORD passes through to strike Egypt and sees the blood on the lintel and the two doorposts, he will pass over the door and not let the destroyer enter your houses to strike you.

[24] "Keep this command permanently as a statute for you and your descendants. [25] When you enter the land that the LORD will give you as he promised, you are to observe this ceremony. [26] When your children ask you, 'What does this ceremony mean to you?' [27] you are to reply, 'It is the Passover sacrifice to the LORD, for he passed over the houses of the Israelites in Egypt when he struck the Egyptians, and he spared our homes.'" So the people knelt low and worshiped. [28] Then the Israelites went and did this; they did just as the LORD had commanded Moses and Aaron.

# THE SABBATH *and* RESURRECTION SUNDAY

*[We] have come to the possession of a new hope, no longer observing the Sabbath, but living in the observance of the Lord's day, on which also our life has sprung up again by him and by his death.*

*IGNATIUS OF ANTIOCH, AD 110*

---

Again and again, the New Testament boldly proclaims that Jesus Christ's triumphant resurrection—displaying His power over death—was an event unlike any other the world has ever known. Resurrection Sunday changed every aspect of life for Jesus's followers, including the day of the week when they worshiped.

For centuries, the Jewish people gathered in worship to observe the Sabbath from sundown on Friday to sundown on Saturday. The marking of the Sabbath was instituted at creation and reinforced by the Ten Commandments. However, after Jesus conquered the grave by His resurrection, converts to Christianity began joining together to worship on Sundays.

The last four days of this Mark reading plan intentionally mirror the rhythm of the first Easter weekend to honor and mark the power of the resurrection. No matter where you are in the calendar year, we invite you to reflect and remember this holy weekend in real time as you read.

# JESUS PRAYS IN THE GARDEN

## *DAY 18*

MARK 14:17–52

BETRAYAL AT THE PASSOVER

[17] When evening came, he arrived with the Twelve. [18] While they were reclining and eating, Jesus said, "Truly I tell you, one of you will betray me—one who is eating with me."

[19] They began to be distressed and to say to him one by one, "Surely not I?"

[20] He said to them, "It is one of the Twelve—the one who is dipping bread in the bowl with me. [21] For the Son of Man will go just as it is written about him, but woe to that man by whom the Son of Man is betrayed! It would have been better for him if he had not been born."

THE FIRST LORD'S SUPPER

[22] As they were eating, he took bread, blessed and broke it, gave it to them, and said, "Take it; this is my body." [23] Then he took a cup, and after giving thanks, he gave it to them, and they all drank from it.

*[24] He said to them, "This is my blood of the covenant, which is poured out for many.*

[25] Truly I tell you, I will no longer drink of the fruit of the vine until that day when I drink it new in the kingdom of God."

[26] After singing a hymn, they went out to the Mount of Olives.

## MARKAN SANDWICH

*MARK 14:17–31*

**Opens with**

Jesus predicting one of His disciples will betray Him.

**Shifts to**

Jesus instituting the Lord's Supper.

**Returns to**

Jesus predicting Peter's denial.

PETER'S DENIAL PREDICTED

[27] Then Jesus said to them, "All of you will fall away, because it is written:

I will strike the shepherd,
and the sheep will be scattered.

[28] But after I have risen, I will go ahead of you to Galilee."

[29] Peter told him, "Even if everyone falls away, I will not."

[30] "Truly I tell you," Jesus said to him, "today, this very night, before the rooster crows twice, you will deny me three times."

[31] But he kept insisting, "If I have to die with you, I will never deny you." And they all said the same thing.

THE PRAYER IN THE GARDEN

[32] Then they came to a place named Gethsemane, and he told his disciples, "Sit here while I pray." [33] He took Peter, James, and John with him, and he began to be deeply distressed and troubled. [34] He said to them, "I am deeply grieved to the point of death. Remain here and stay awake."

*[35] He went a little farther, fell to the ground, and prayed that if it were possible, the hour might pass from him.*

[36] And he said, "*Abba*, Father! All things are possible for you. Take this cup away from me. Nevertheless, not what I will, but what you will." [37] Then he came and found them sleeping. He said to Peter, "Simon, are you sleeping? Couldn't you stay awake one hour? [38] Stay awake and pray so that you won't enter into temptation. The spirit is willing, but the flesh is weak." [39] Once again he went away and prayed, saying the same thing. [40] And again he came and found them sleeping, because they could not keep their eyes open. They did not know what to say to him. [41] Then he came a third time and said to them, "Are you still sleeping and resting? Enough! The time has come. See, the Son of Man is betrayed into the hands of sinners. [42] Get up; let's go. See, my betrayer is near."

JUDAS'S BETRAYAL OF JESUS

[43] While he was still speaking, Judas, one of the Twelve, suddenly arrived. With him was a mob, with swords and clubs, from the chief priests, the scribes, and the elders. [44] His betrayer had given them a signal. "The one I kiss," he said, "he's the one; arrest him and take him away under guard." [45] So when he came, immediately

he went up to Jesus and said, "Rabbi!" and kissed him. [46] They took hold of him and arrested him. [47] One of those who stood by drew his sword, struck the high priest's servant, and cut off his ear.

[48] Jesus said to them, "Have you come out with swords and clubs, as if I were a criminal, to capture me? [49] Every day I was among you, teaching in the temple, and you didn't arrest me.

*But the Scriptures must be fulfilled."*

[50] Then they all deserted him and ran away. [51] Now a certain young man, wearing nothing but a linen cloth, was following him. They caught hold of him, [52] but he left the linen cloth behind and ran away naked.

HEBREWS 5:7–8

[7] During his earthly life, he offered prayers and appeals with loud cries and tears to the one who was able to save him from death, and he was heard because of his reverence.

*[8] Although he was the Son, he learned obedience from what he suffered.*

# JESUS GIVES HIS LIFE

## *DAY 19*

MARK 14:53–72

JESUS FACES THE SANHEDRIN

[53] They led Jesus away to the high priest, and all the chief priests, the elders, and the scribes assembled. [54] Peter followed him at a distance, right into the high priest's courtyard. He was sitting with the servants, warming himself by the fire.

[55] The chief priests and the whole Sanhedrin were looking for testimony against Jesus to put him to death, but they could not find any. [56] For many were giving false testimony against him, and the testimonies did not agree. [57] Some stood up and gave false testimony against him, stating, [58] "We heard him say, 'I will destroy this temple made with human hands, and in three days I will build another not made by hands.'" [59] Yet their testimony did not agree even on this.

[60] Then the high priest stood up before them all and questioned Jesus, "Don't you have an answer to what these men are testifying against you?" [61] But he kept silent and did not answer. Again the high priest questioned him, "Are you the Messiah, the Son of the Blessed One?"

[62] "I am," said Jesus, "and you will see the Son of Man seated at the right hand of Power and coming with the clouds of heaven."

[63] Then the high priest tore his robes and said, "Why do we still need witnesses? [64] You have heard the blasphemy. What is your decision?" They all condemned him as deserving death.

[65] Then some began to spit on him, to blindfold him, and to beat him, saying, "Prophesy!" The temple servants also took him and slapped him.

### PETER DENIES HIS LORD

[66] While Peter was in the courtyard below, one of the high priest's maidservants came. [67] When she saw Peter warming himself, she looked at him and said, "You also were with Jesus, the man from Nazareth."

[68] But he denied it: "I don't know or understand what you're talking about." Then he went out to the entryway, and a rooster crowed.

[69] When the maidservant saw him again, she began to tell those standing nearby, "This man is one of them."

[70] But again he denied it. After a little while those standing there said to Peter again, "You certainly are one of them, since you're also a Galilean."

[71] Then he started to curse and swear, "I don't know this man you're talking about!"

[72] Immediately a rooster crowed a second time, and Peter remembered when Jesus had spoken the word to him, "Before the rooster crows twice, you will deny me three times." And he broke down and wept.

## MARK 15:1–41

### JESUS FACES PILATE

[1] As soon as it was morning, having held a meeting with the elders, scribes, and the whole Sanhedrin, the chief priests tied Jesus up, led him away, and handed him over to Pilate.

[2] So Pilate asked him, "Are you the king of the Jews?"

He answered him, "You say so."

[3] And the chief priests accused him of many things. [4] Pilate questioned him again, "Aren't you going to answer? Look how many things they are accusing you of!" [5] But Jesus still did not answer, and so Pilate was amazed.

### JESUS OR BARABBAS

[6] At the festival Pilate used to release for the people a prisoner whom they requested. [7] There was one named Barabbas, who was in prison with rebels who

had committed murder during the rebellion. [8] The crowd came up and began to ask Pilate to do for them as was his custom. [9] Pilate answered them, "Do you want me to release the king of the Jews for you?" [10] For he knew it was because of envy that the chief priests had handed him over. [11] But the chief priests stirred up the crowd so that he would release Barabbas to them instead. [12] Pilate asked them again, "Then what do you want me to do with the one you call the king of the Jews?"

## [13] *Again they shouted, "Crucify him!"*

[14] Pilate said to them, "Why? What has he done wrong?"

But they shouted all the more, "Crucify him!"

[15] Wanting to satisfy the crowd, Pilate released Barabbas to them; and after having Jesus flogged, he handed him over to be crucified.

### MOCKED BY THE MILITARY

[16] The soldiers led him away into the palace (that is, the governor's residence) and called the whole company together. [17] They dressed him in a purple robe, twisted together a crown of thorns, and put it on him. [18] And they began to salute him, "Hail, king of the Jews!" [19] They were hitting him on the head with a stick and spitting on him. Getting down on their knees, they were paying him homage. [20] After they had mocked him, they stripped him of the purple robe and put his clothes on him.

### CRUCIFIED BETWEEN TWO CRIMINALS

They led him out to crucify him. [21] They forced a man coming in from the country, who was passing by, to carry Jesus's cross. He was Simon of Cyrene, the father of Alexander and Rufus.

[22] They brought Jesus to the place called *Golgotha* (which means Place of the Skull). [23] They tried to give him wine mixed with myrrh, but he did not take it.

[24] Then they crucified him and divided his clothes, casting lots for them to decide what each would get. [25] Now it was nine in the morning when they crucified him. [26] The inscription of the charge written against him was: THE KING OF THE JEWS [27] They crucified two criminals with him, one on his right and one on his left.

[29] Those who passed by were yelling insults at him, shaking their heads, and saying, "Ha! The one who would destroy the temple and rebuild it in three days, [30] save

yourself by coming down from the cross!" [31] In the same way, the chief priests with the scribes were mocking him among themselves and saying, "He saved others, but he cannot save himself! [32] Let the Messiah, the King of Israel, come down now from the cross, so that we may see and believe." Even those who were crucified with him taunted him.

### THE DEATH OF JESUS

[33] When it was noon, darkness came over the whole land until three in the afternoon. [34] And at three Jesus cried out with a loud voice, *"Eloi, Eloi, lemá sabachtháni?"* which is translated, "My God, my God, why have you abandoned me?"

[35] When some of those standing there heard this, they said, "See, he's calling for Elijah."

[36] Someone ran and filled a sponge with sour wine, fixed it on a stick, offered him a drink, and said, "Let's see if Elijah comes to take him down."

[37] Jesus let out a loud cry and breathed his last. [38] Then the curtain of the temple was torn in two from top to bottom. [39] When the centurion, who was standing opposite him, saw the way he breathed his last, he said,

*"Truly this man was the Son of God!"*

[40] There were also women watching from a distance. Among them were Mary Magdalene, Mary the mother of James the younger and of Joses, and Salome. [41] In Galilee these women followed him and took care of him. Many other women had come up with him to Jerusalem.

## PSALM 38:20–22

[20] Those who repay evil for good
attack me for pursuing good.

[21] LORD, do not abandon me;
my God, do not be far from me.
[22] Hurry to help me,
my Lord, my salvation.

ISAIAH 53:2–3

[2] He grew up before him like a young plant
and like a root out of dry ground.

*He didn't have an impressive form*
*or majesty that we should look at him,*

no appearance that we should desire him.
[3] He was despised and rejected by men,
a man of suffering who knew what sickness was.
He was like someone people turned away from;
he was despised, and we didn't value him.

DAY 20

# THE BURIAL OF JESUS

## MARK 15:42–47

### THE BURIAL OF JESUS

[42] When it was already evening, because it was the day of preparation (that is, the day before the Sabbath), [43] Joseph of Arimathea, a prominent member of the Sanhedrin who was himself looking forward to the kingdom of God, came and boldly went to Pilate and asked for Jesus's body. [44] Pilate was surprised that he was already dead. Summoning the centurion, he asked him whether he had already died. [45] When he found out from the centurion, he gave the corpse to Joseph. [46] After he bought some linen cloth, Joseph took him down and wrapped him in the linen. Then he laid him in a tomb cut out of the rock and rolled a stone against the entrance to the tomb. [47] Mary Magdalene and Mary the mother of Joses were watching where he was laid.

## LAMENTATIONS 3:1–9, 19–24

### HOPE THROUGH GOD'S MERCY

ALEPH

[1] I am the man who has seen affliction
under the rod of God's wrath.
[2] He has driven me away and forced me to walk
in darkness instead of light.
[3] Yes, he repeatedly turns his hand
against me all day long.

BETH

[4] He has worn away my flesh and skin;
he has broken my bones.
[5] He has laid siege against me,
encircling me with bitterness and hardship.
[6] He has made me dwell in darkness
like those who have been dead for ages.

GIMEL

[7] He has walled me in so I cannot get out;
he has weighed me down with chains.
[8] Even when I cry out and plead for help,
he blocks out my prayer.
[9] He has walled in my ways with blocks of stone;
he has made my paths crooked.

. . .

ZAYIN

[19] Remember my affliction and my homelessness,
the wormwood and the poison.
[20] I continually remember them
and have become depressed.
[21] Yet I call this to mind,
and therefore I have hope:

CHETH

[22] Because of the LORD's faithful love
we do not perish,
for his mercies never end.
[23] They are new every morning;
great is your faithfulness!
[24] I say, "The LORD is my portion,
therefore I will put my hope in him."

## COLOSSIANS 1:15–23

### THE CENTRALITY OF CHRIST

[15] He is the image of the invisible God,
the firstborn over all creation.
[16] For everything was created by him,
in heaven and on earth,
the visible and the invisible,
whether thrones or dominions
or rulers or authorities—
all things have been created through him and for him.
[17] He is before all things,
and by him all things hold together.
[18] He is also the head of the body, the church;
he is the beginning,
the firstborn from the dead,
so that he might come to have
first place in everything.
[19] For God was pleased to have
all his fullness dwell in him,
[20] and through him to reconcile
everything to himself,
whether things on earth or things in heaven,
by making peace
through his blood, shed on the cross.

[21] Once you were alienated and hostile in your minds as expressed in your evil actions. [22] But now he has reconciled you by his physical body through his death, to present you holy, faultless, and blameless before him— [23] if indeed you remain grounded and steadfast in the faith and are not shifted away from the hope of the gospel that you heard. This gospel has been proclaimed in all creation under heaven, and I, Paul, have become a servant of it.

*WORDS* ST. 1, 2, EDWARD PERRONET; ST. 3, 4, JOHN RIPPON

# ALL HAIL *the* POWER *of* JESUS'S NAME

*MUSIC* OLIVER HOLDEN

1. All hail the power of Je - sus's name! Let an - gels pros - trate
2. Ye cho - sen seed of Is - rael's race, Ye ran - somed from the
3. Let ev - 'ry kin - dred, ev - 'ry tribe on this ter - res - trial
4. O that with yon - der sa - cred throng we at His feet may
fall; Bring forth the roy - al di - a - dem, And
fall, Hail Him who saves you by His grace, And
ball, To Him all maj - es - ty as - cribe, And
fall! We'll join the ev - er - last - ing song, And
crown Him Lord of all; Bring forth the roy - al
crown Him Lord of all; Hail Him who saves you
crown Him Lord of all; To Him all maj - es -
crown Him Lord of all; We'll join the ev - er -
di - a - dem, And crown Him Lord of all.
by His grace, And crown Him Lord of all.
ty as - cribe, And crown Him Lord of all.
last - ing song, And crown Him Lord of all.

# RESURRECTION MORNING

*DAY 21*

## MARK 16

### RESURRECTION MORNING

[1] When the Sabbath was over, Mary Magdalene, Mary the mother of James, and Salome bought spices, so that they could go and anoint him. [2] Very early in the morning, on the first day of the week, they went to the tomb at sunrise. [3] They were saying to one another, "Who will roll away the stone from the entrance to the tomb for us?" [4] Looking up, they noticed that the stone—which was very large—had been rolled away.

[5] When they entered the tomb, they saw a young man dressed in a white robe sitting on the right side; they were alarmed. [6] "Don't be alarmed," he told them.

*"You are looking for Jesus of Nazareth, who was crucified. He has risen!*

He is not here. See the place where they put him. [7] But go, tell his disciples and Peter, 'He is going ahead of you to Galilee; you will see him there just as he told you.'"

[8] They went out and ran from the tomb, because trembling and astonishment overwhelmed them. And they said nothing to anyone, since they were afraid.

*[Some of the earliest manuscripts conclude with 16:8.]*

### THE LONGER ENDING OF MARK: APPEARANCES OF THE RISEN LORD

[[9] Early on the first day of the week, after he had risen, he appeared first to Mary Magdalene, out of whom he had driven seven demons. [10] She went and reported to those who had been with him, as they were mourning and weeping. [11] Yet, when they heard that he was alive and had been seen by her, they did not believe it.

[12] After this, he appeared in a different form to two of them walking on their way into the country. [13] And they went and reported it to the rest, who did not believe them either.

### THE GREAT COMMISSION

[14] Later he appeared to the Eleven themselves as they were reclining at the table. He rebuked their unbelief and hardness of heart, because they did not believe those who saw him after he had risen. [15] Then he said to them,

*"Go into all the world and preach the gospel to all creation.*

[16] Whoever believes and is baptized will be saved, but whoever does not believe will be condemned. [17] And these signs will accompany those who believe: In my name they will drive out demons; they will speak in new tongues; [18] they will pick up snakes; if they should drink anything deadly, it will not harm them; they will lay hands on the sick, and they will get well."

### THE ASCENSION

[19] So the Lord Jesus, after speaking to them, was taken up into heaven and sat down at the right hand of God. [20] And they went out and preached everywhere, while the Lord worked with them and confirmed the word by the accompanying signs.]

## 1 CORINTHIANS 15:12–28, 50–58

### RESURRECTION ESSENTIAL TO THE FAITH

[12] Now if Christ is proclaimed as raised from the dead, how can some of you say, "There is no resurrection of the dead"? [13] If there is no resurrection of the dead, then not even Christ has been raised; [14] and if Christ has not been raised, then our proclamation is in vain, and so is your faith. [15] Moreover, we are found to be false witnesses about God, because we have testified wrongly about God that he raised up Christ—whom he did not raise up, if in fact the dead are not raised. [16] For if the dead are not raised, not even Christ has been raised. [17] And if Christ has not been raised, your faith is worthless; you are still in your sins. [18] Those, then, who have fallen asleep in Christ have also perished. [19] If we have put our hope in Christ for this life only, we should be pitied more than anyone.

CHRIST'S RESURRECTION GUARANTEES OURS

[20] But as it is, Christ has been raised from the dead, the firstfruits of those who have fallen asleep. [21] For since death came through a man, the resurrection of the dead also comes through a man. [22] For just as in Adam all die, so also in Christ all will be made alive.

[23] But each in his own order: Christ, the firstfruits; afterward, at his coming, those who belong to Christ. [24] Then comes the end, when he hands over the kingdom to God the Father, when he abolishes all rule and all authority and power. [25] For he must reign until he puts all his enemies under his feet. [26] The last enemy to be abolished is death. [27] For God has put everything under his feet. Now when it says "everything" is put under him, it is obvious that he who puts everything under him is the exception. [28] When everything is subject to Christ, then the Son himself will also be subject to the one who subjected everything to him, so that God may be all in all.

...

VICTORIOUS RESURRECTION

[50] What I am saying, brothers and sisters, is this: Flesh and blood cannot inherit the kingdom of God, nor can corruption inherit incorruption. [51] Listen, I am telling you a mystery: We will not all fall asleep, but we will all be changed, [52] in a moment, in the twinkling of an eye, at the last trumpet. For the trumpet will sound, and the dead will be raised incorruptible, and we will be changed. [53] For this corruptible body must be clothed with incorruptibility, and this mortal body must be clothed with immortality. [54] When this corruptible body is clothed with incorruptibility, and this mortal body is clothed with immortality, then the saying that is written will take place:

Death has been swallowed up in victory.
[55] Where, death, is your victory?
Where, death, is your sting?

[56] The sting of death is sin, and the power of sin is the law. [57] But thanks be to God, who gives us the victory through our Lord Jesus Christ!

[58] Therefore, my dear brothers and sisters, be steadfast, immovable, always excelling in the Lord's work, because you know that your labor in the Lord is not in vain.

## REVELATION 21:3–4

[3] Then I heard a loud voice from the throne: Look, God's dwelling is with humanity, and he will live with them. They will be his peoples, and God himself will be with them and will be their God. [4] He will wipe away every tear from their eyes. Death will be no more; grief, crying, and pain will be no more, because the previous things have passed away.

# WEEK *3*
## *Reflection*

Jesus's earthly ministry culminated in His death on the cross and His resurrection from the grave. Look back over this week's reading and reflect on Jesus's humanity and divinity shown in the events of Holy Week.

THE ANOINTING *at* BETHANY — *DAY 17*

THE LORD'S SUPPER — *DAY 18*

THE PRAYER *in the* GARDEN — *DAY 18*

JUDAS'S BETRAYAL — *DAY 18*

BEFORE *the* SANHEDRIN — *DAY 19*

PETER'S DENIAL — *DAY 19*

ENCOUNTER *with* PILATE — *DAY 19*

THE CRUCIFIXION — *DAY 19*

THE RESURRECTION — *DAY 21*

THE GREAT COMMISSION — *DAY 21*

THE ASCENSION — *DAY 21*

YOU ARE LOOKING FOR JESUS OF NAZARETH, WHO WAS CRUCIFIED. HE HAS RISEN!

Reflect on all Christ endured on the cross and overcame by His resurrection. Use the journaling space below to respond to the life, death, and resurrection of Jesus. Write a prayer of thankfulness for how His work offers you redemption and restoration.

# BENEDICTION

*"The time is fulfilled, and the kingdom of God has come near. Repent and believe the good news!"*

*MARK 1:15*

## CSB BOOK ABBREVIATIONS

OLD TESTAMENT

**GN** Genesis
**EX** Exodus
**LV** Leviticus
**NM** Numbers
**DT** Deuteronomy
**JOS** Joshua
**JDG** Judges
**RU** Ruth
**1SM** 1 Samuel
**2SM** 2 Samuel
**1KG** 1 Kings
**2KG** 2 Kings
**1CH** 1 Chronicles
**2CH** 2 Chronicles
**EZR** Ezra
**NEH** Nehemiah
**EST** Esther
**JB** Job
**PS** Psalms
**PR** Proverbs
**EC** Ecclesiastes
**SG** Song of Solomon
**IS** Isaiah
**JR** Jeremiah
**LM** Lamentations
**EZK** Ezekiel
**DN** Daniel
**HS** Hosea
**JL** Joel
**AM** Amos
**OB** Obadiah
**JNH** Jonah
**MC** Micah
**NAH** Nahum
**HAB** Habakkuk
**ZPH** Zephaniah
**HG** Haggai
**ZCH** Zechariah
**MAL** Malachi

NEW TESTAMENT

**MT** Matthew
**MK** Mark
**LK** Luke
**JN** John
**AC** Acts
**RM** Romans
**1CO** 1 Corinthians
**2CO** 2 Corinthians
**GL** Galatians
**EPH** Ephesians
**PHP** Philippians
**COL** Colossians
**1TH** 1 Thessalonians
**2TH** 2 Thessalonians
**1TM** 1 Timothy
**2TM** 2 Timothy
**TI** Titus
**PHM** Philemon
**HEB** Hebrews
**JMS** James
**1PT** 1 Peter
**2PT** 2 Peter
**1JN** 1 John
**2JN** 2 John
**3JN** 3 John
**JD** Jude
**RV** Revelation

---

## BIBLIOGRAPHY


Barry, John D., Douglas Mangum, Derek R. Brown, Michael S. Heiser, Miles Custis, Elliot Ritzema, Matthew M. Whitehead, Michael R. Grigoni, and David Bomar, eds. *Faithlife Study Bible.* Bellingham: Lexham Press, 2016.

Blum, Edwin A., and Trevin Wax, eds. *CSB Study Bible: Notes.* Nashville: Holman Bible Publishers, 2017.

Clendenen, E. Ray, and Jeremy Royal Howard, eds. *Holman Illustrated Bible Commentary.* Nashville: B&H Publishing Group, 2015.

# SHE READS TRUTH PODCAST

**Our podcast supports one simple but powerful mission: Women in the Word of God every day.**

Our hope is that this podcast will serve as a complement to every reading plan, to encourage you on your commute to work, while you're out for a walk, or at home making dinner. God's Word is for you and for now. Join our founders Raechel and Amanda in conversation that delights in the beauty, goodness, and truth found in Scripture. Subscribe today and make it a part of your week!

JOIN US ON APPLE PODCASTS OR YOUR PREFERRED STREAMING PLATFORM

## WHERE DID I STUDY?

- O HOME
- O OFFICE
- O COFFEE SHOP
- O CHURCH
- O A FRIEND'S HOUSE
- O OTHER:

## HOW DID I FIND DELIGHT IN GOD'S WORD?

## WHAT WAS I LISTENING TO?

ARTIST:

SONG:

PLAYLIST:

## WHEN DID I STUDY?

MORNING

AFTERNOON

NIGHT

## WHAT WAS HAPPENING IN MY LIFE?

## WHAT WAS HAPPENING IN THE WORLD?

| MONTH | DAY | YEAR |
| --- | --- | --- |

END DATE